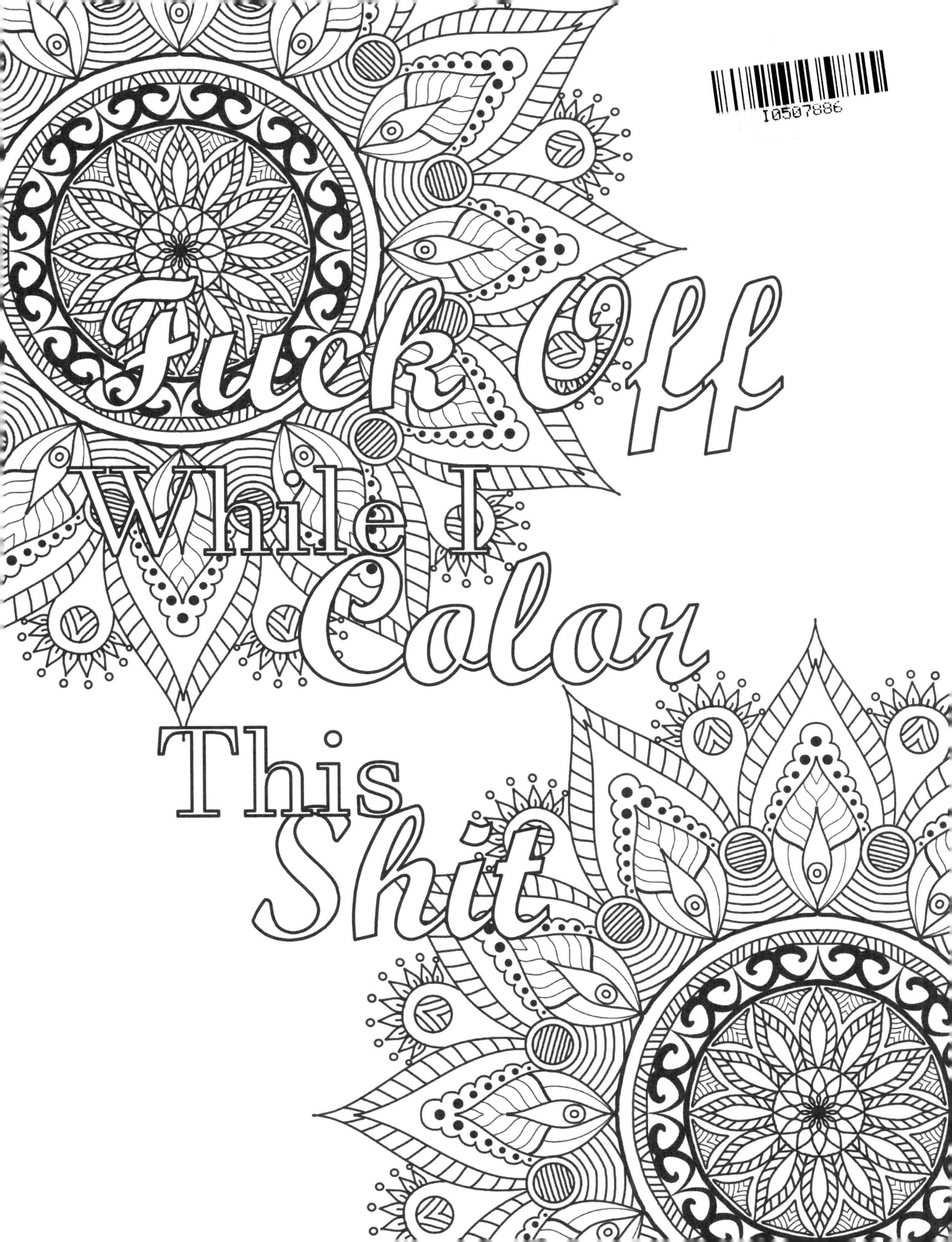

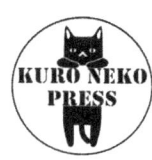 Copyright© Kuro Neko Press
All rights are reserved. No part of this publication may be reproduced, stored in retrieval system, copied in any form or by any means (including electronic, mechanical, photocopying, recording, translating into another language, or otherwise) without prior written permission from the author.

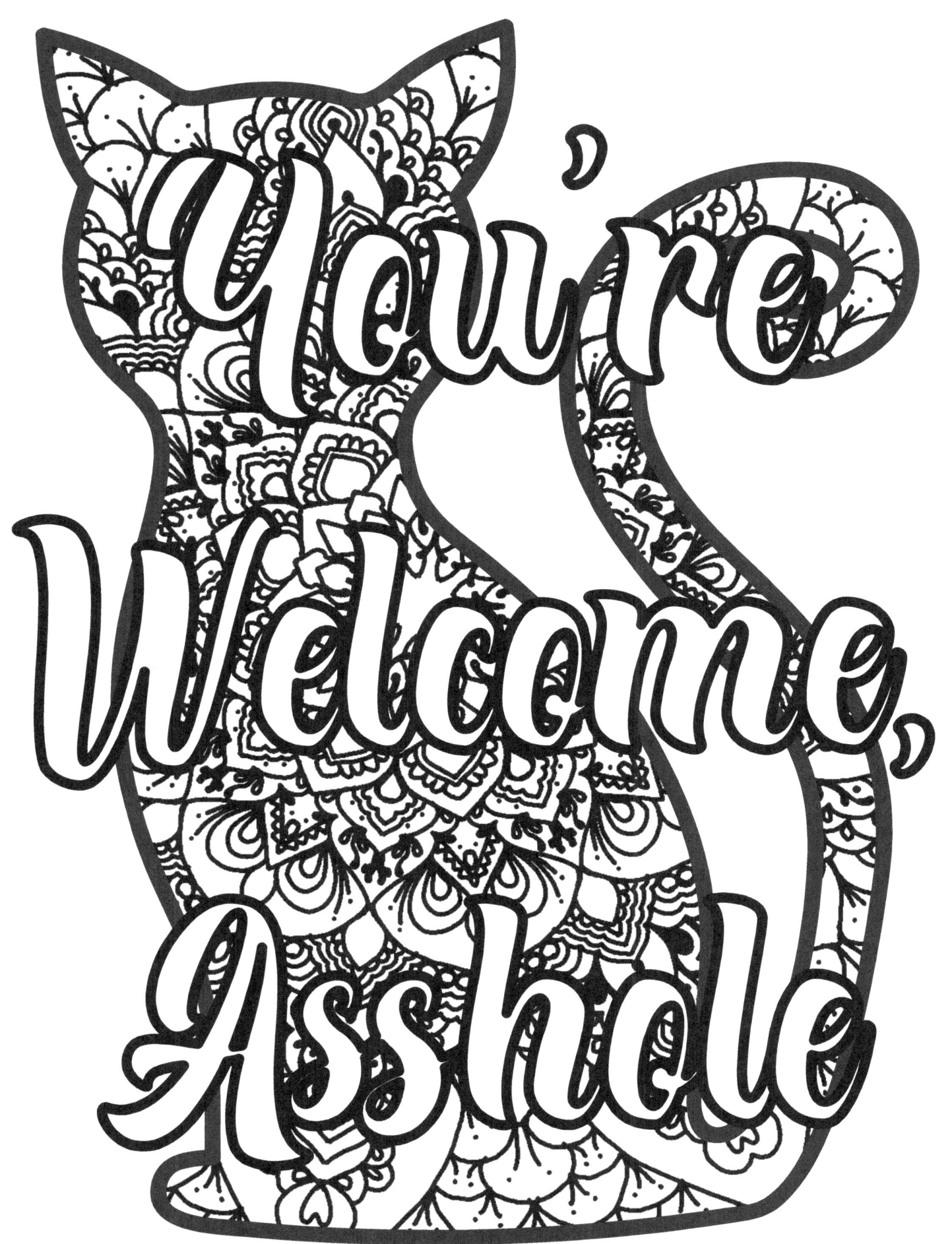

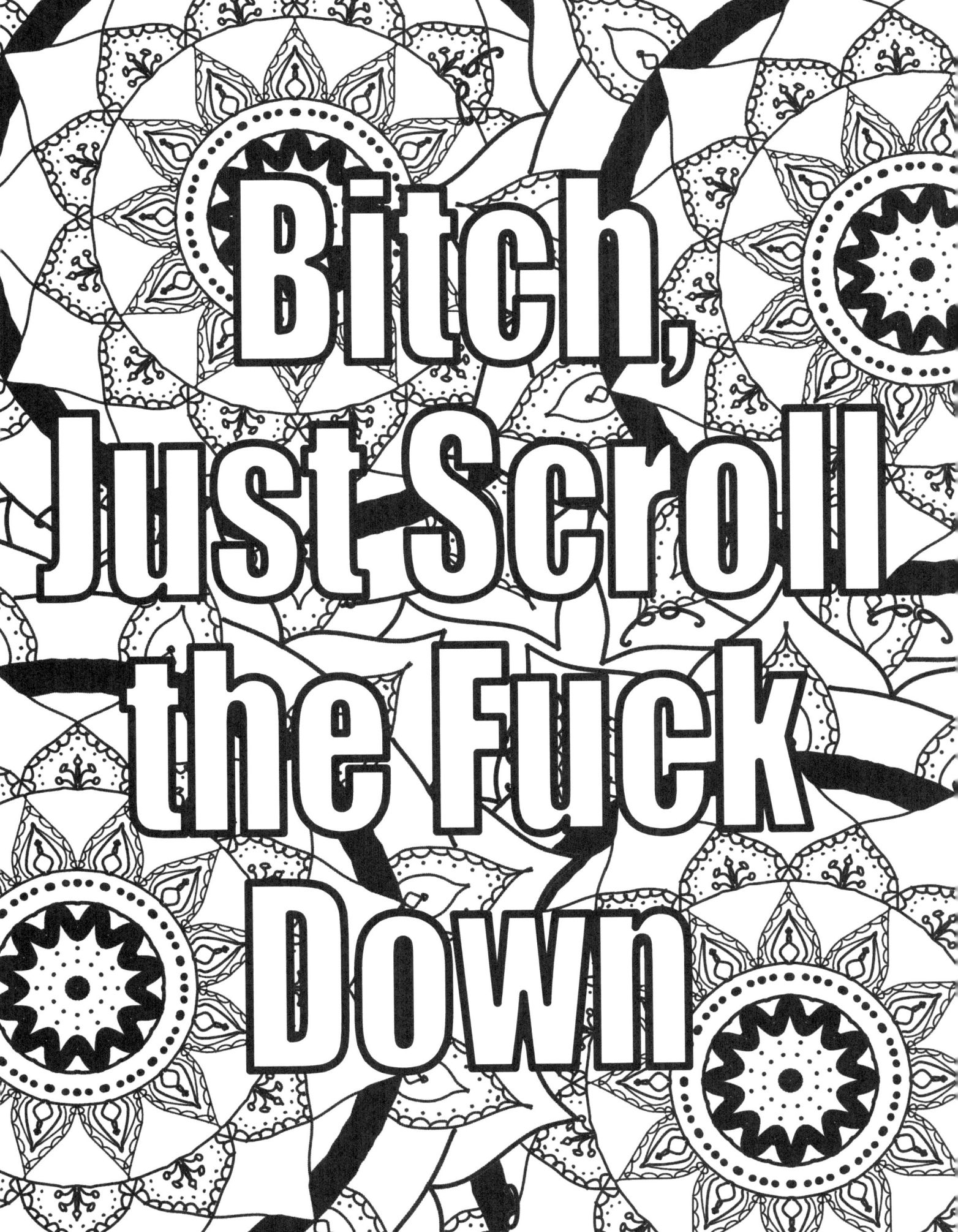

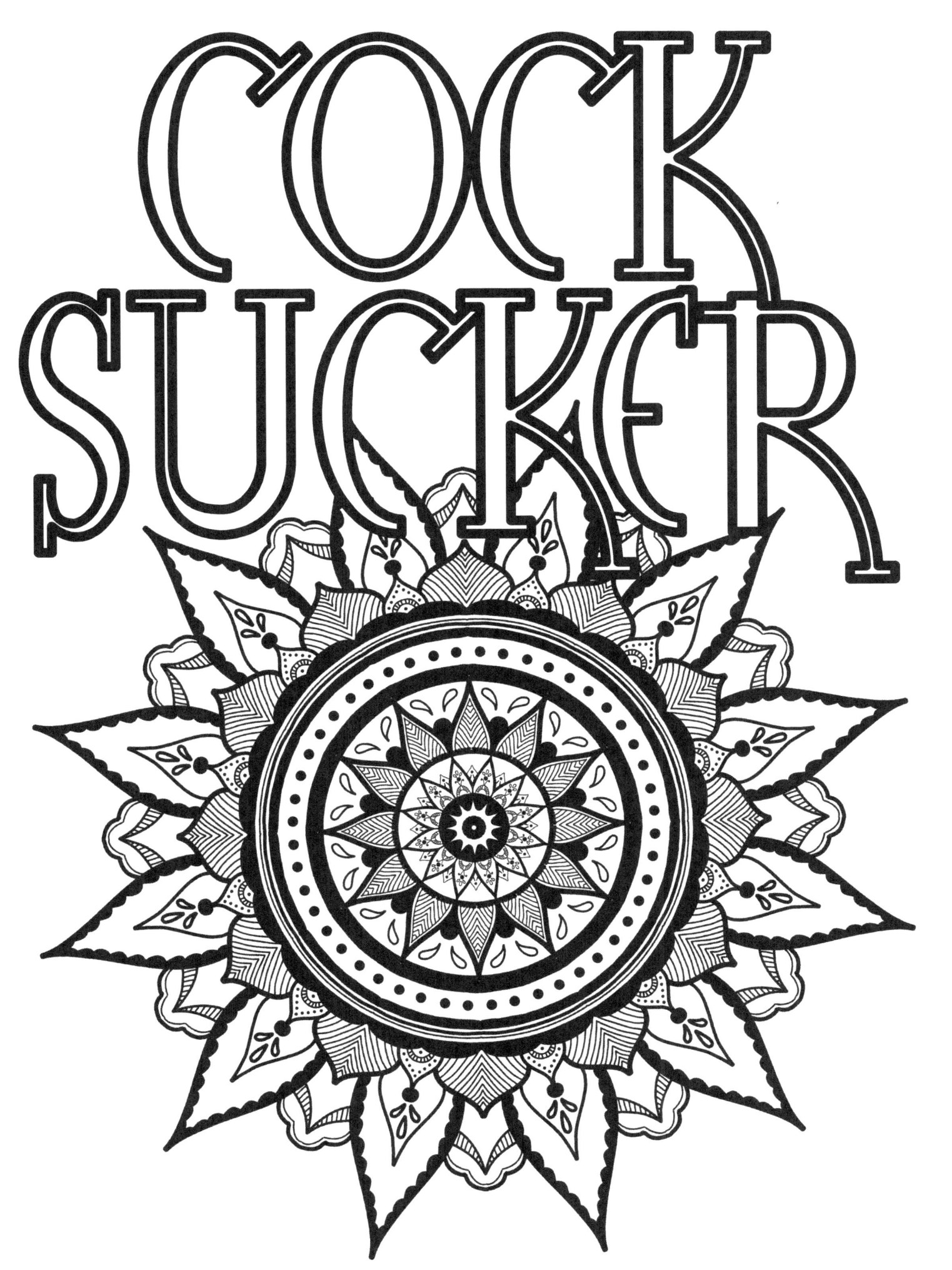

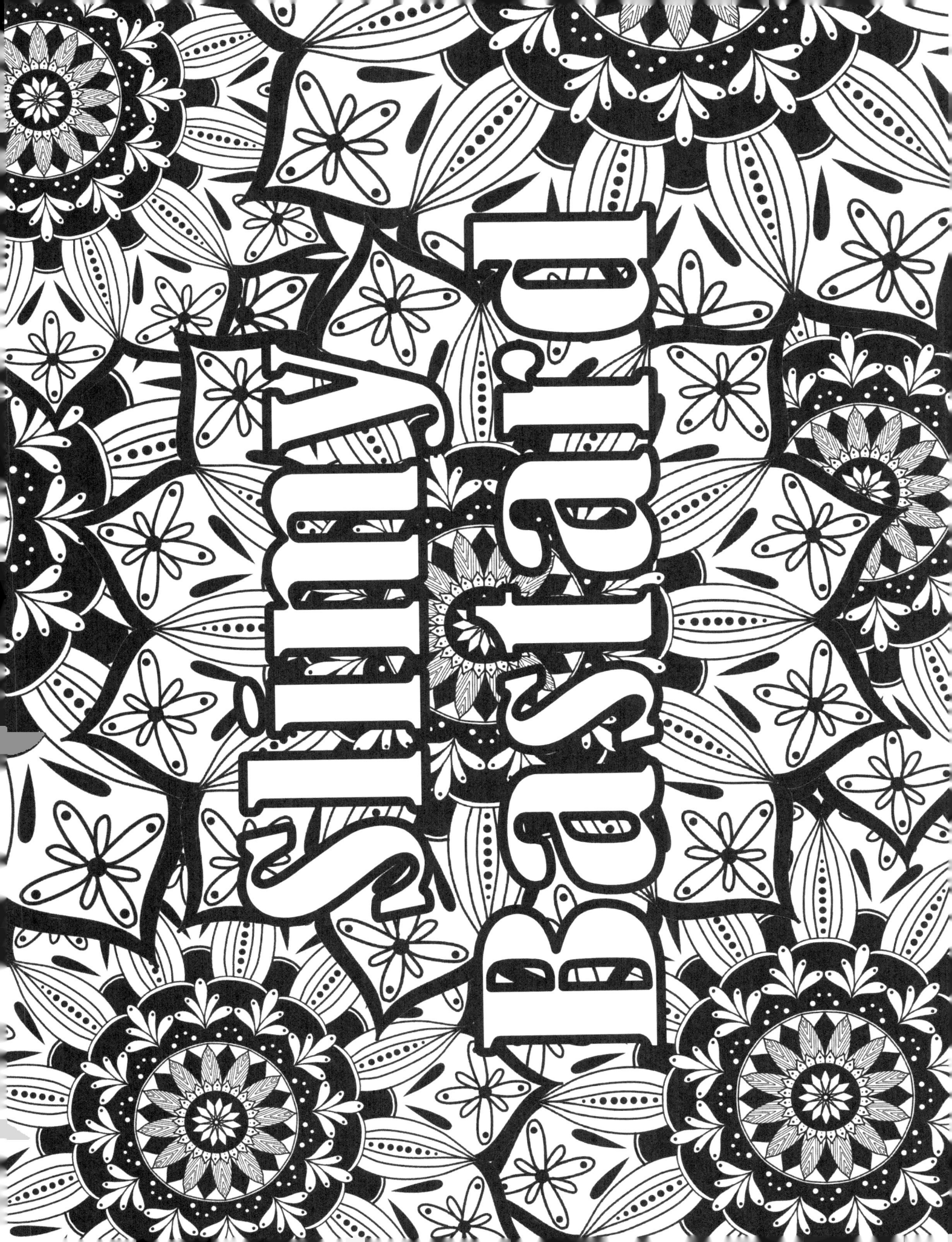

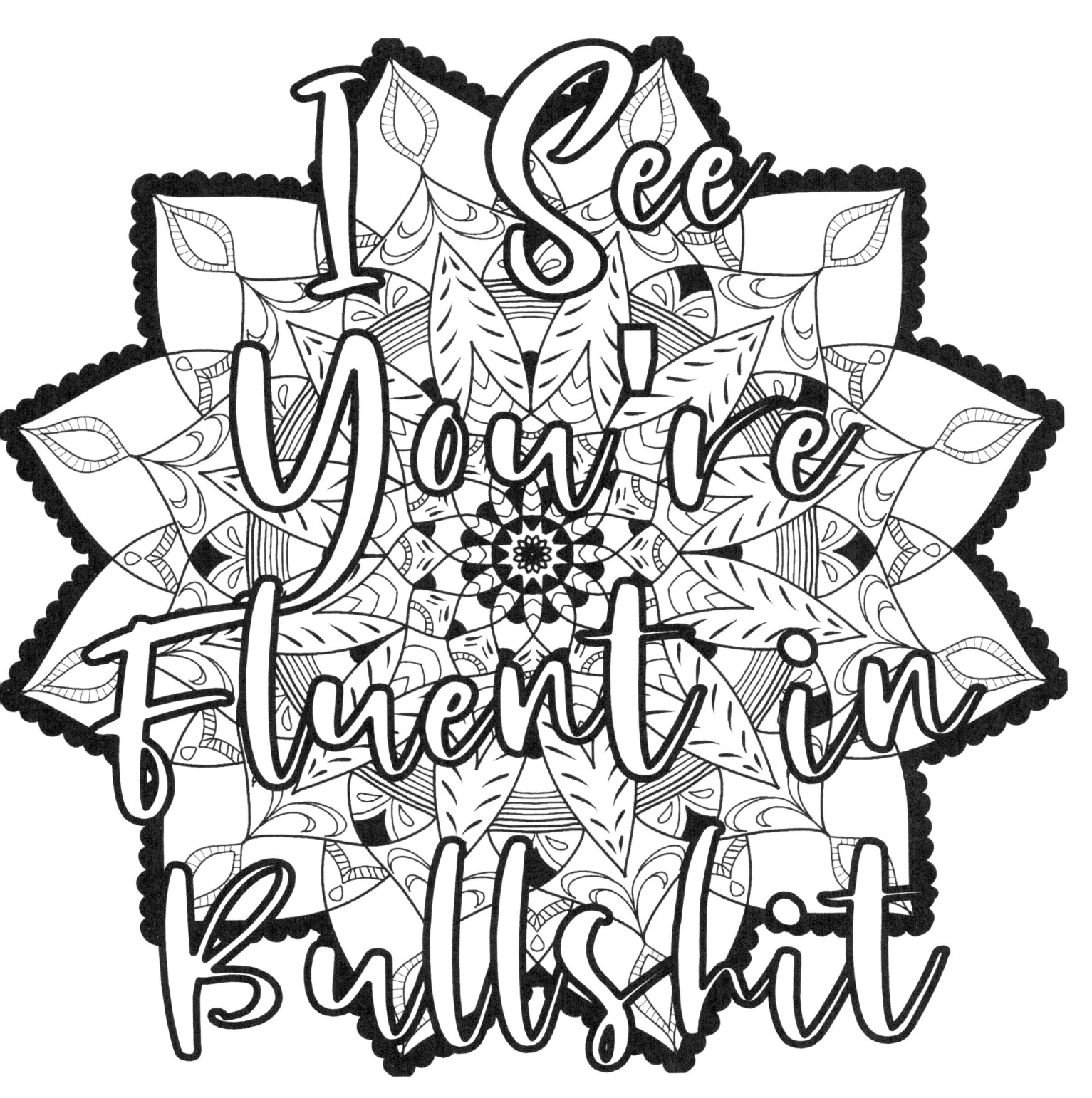

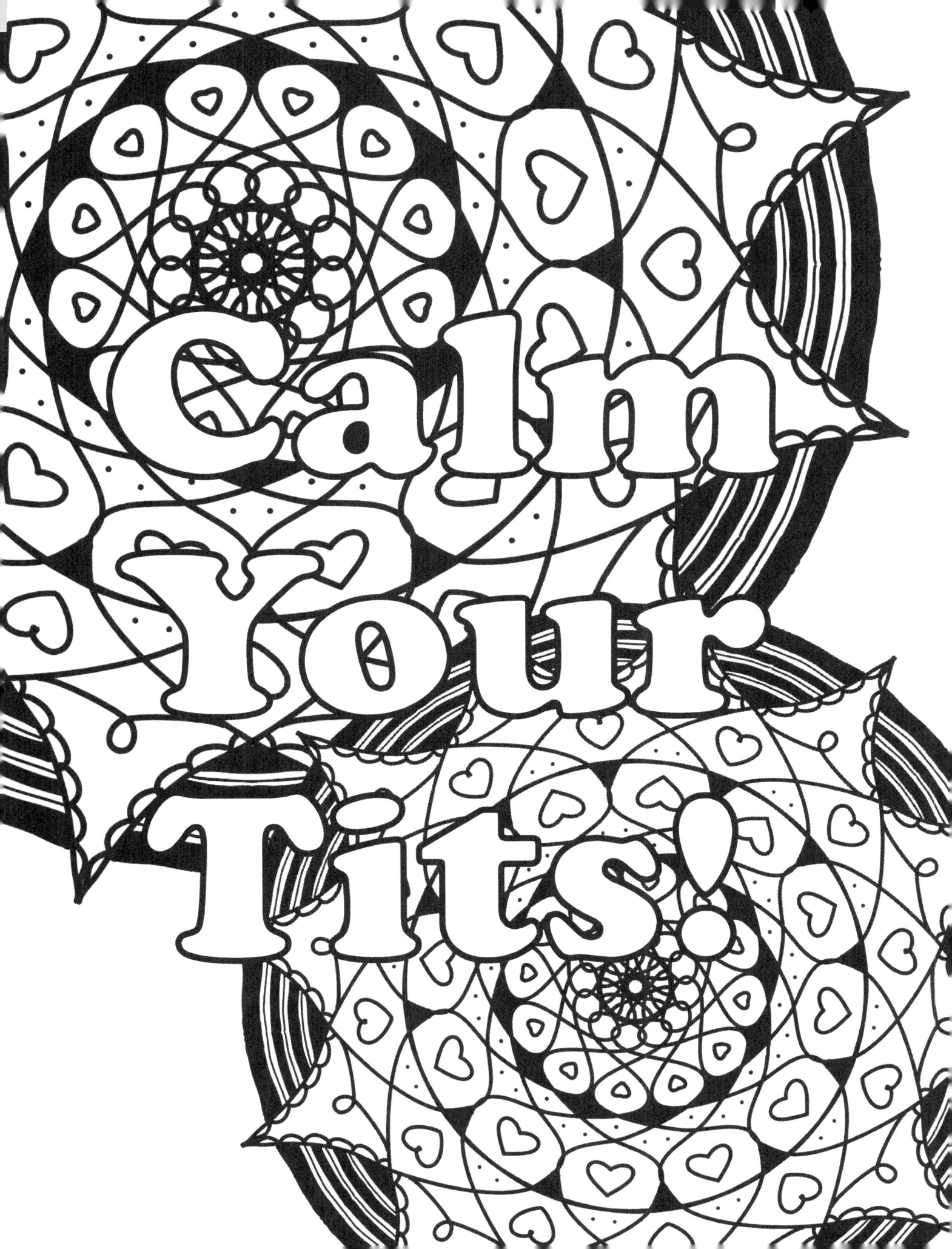

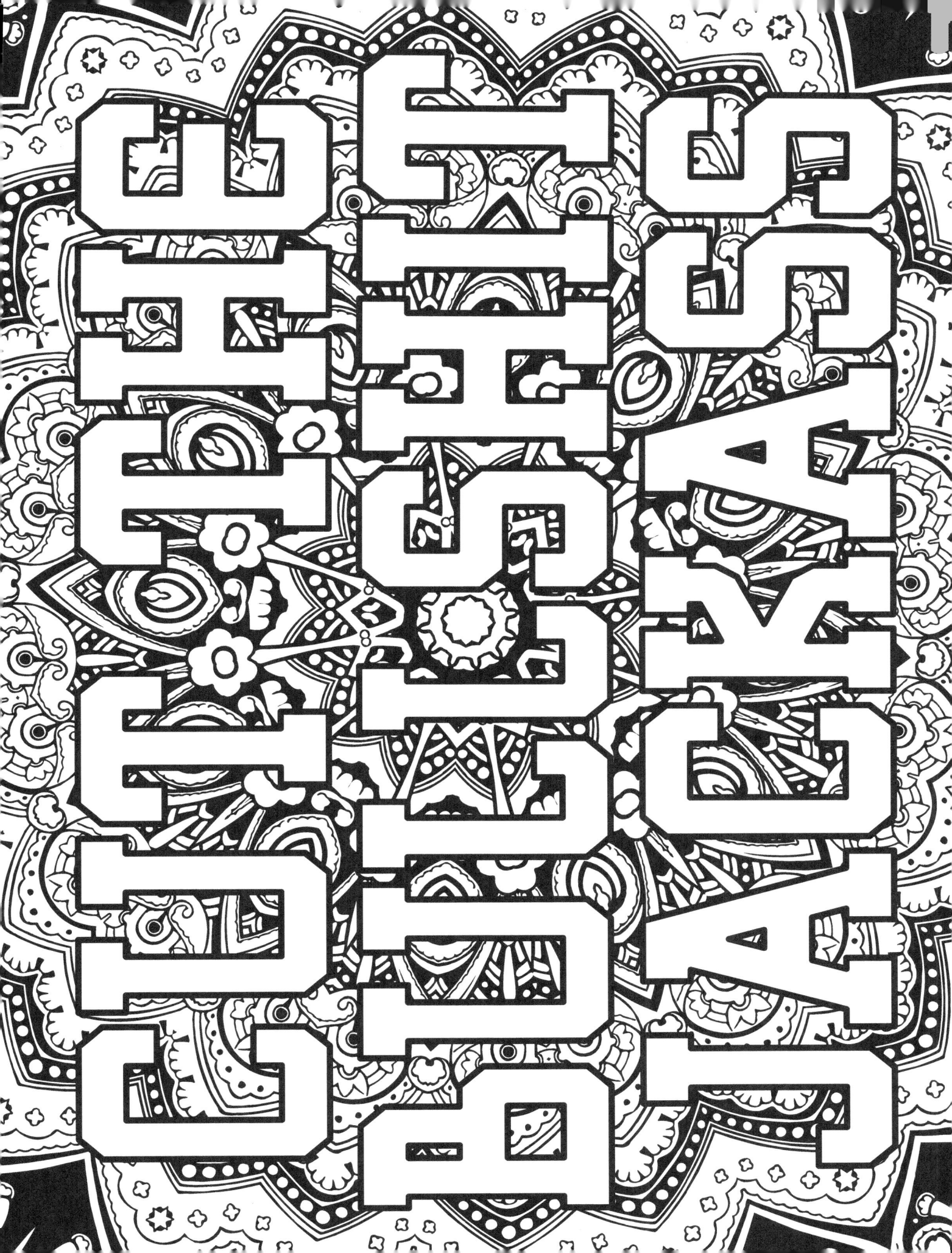

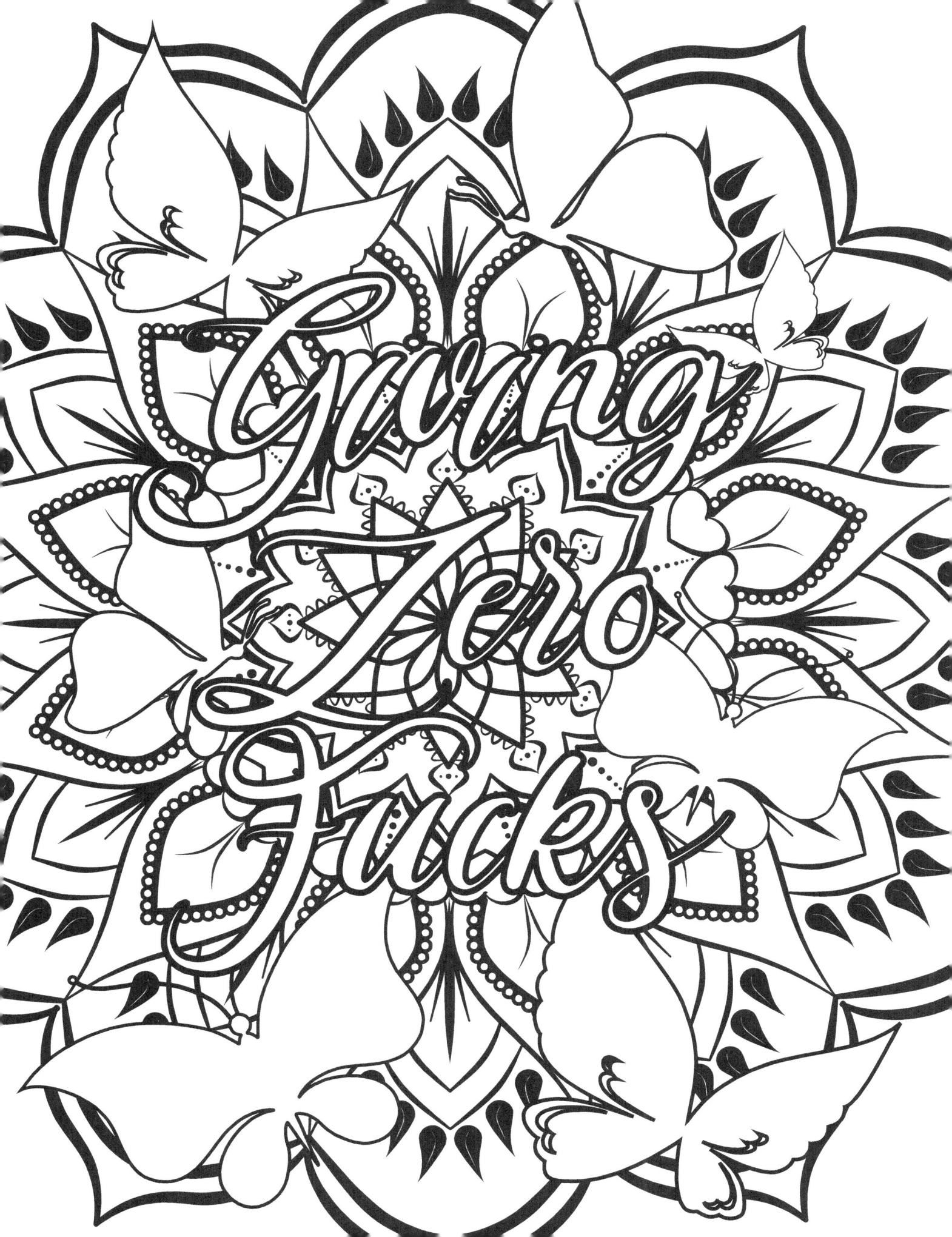

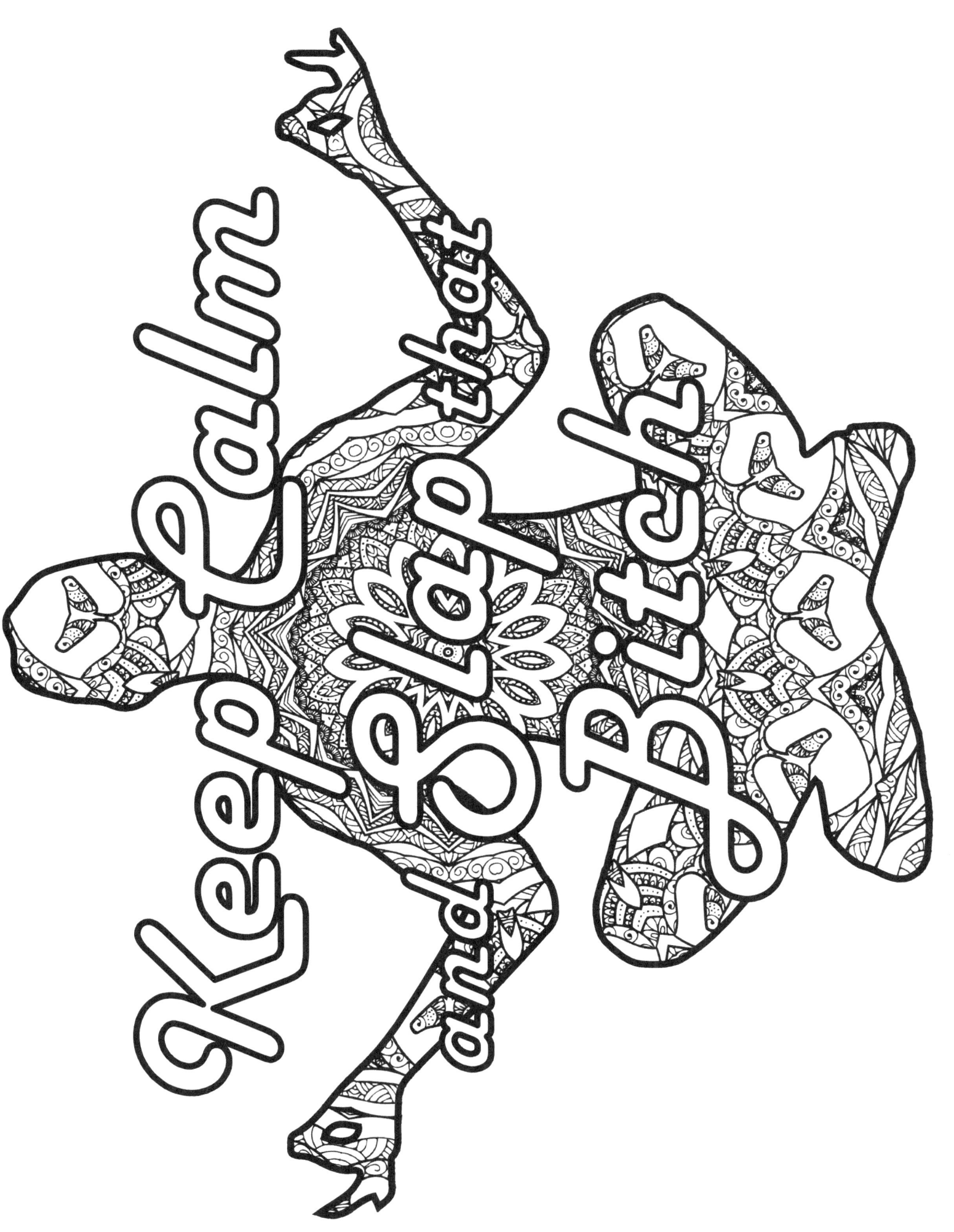

# GET OFF THE ROAD ASSHOLE

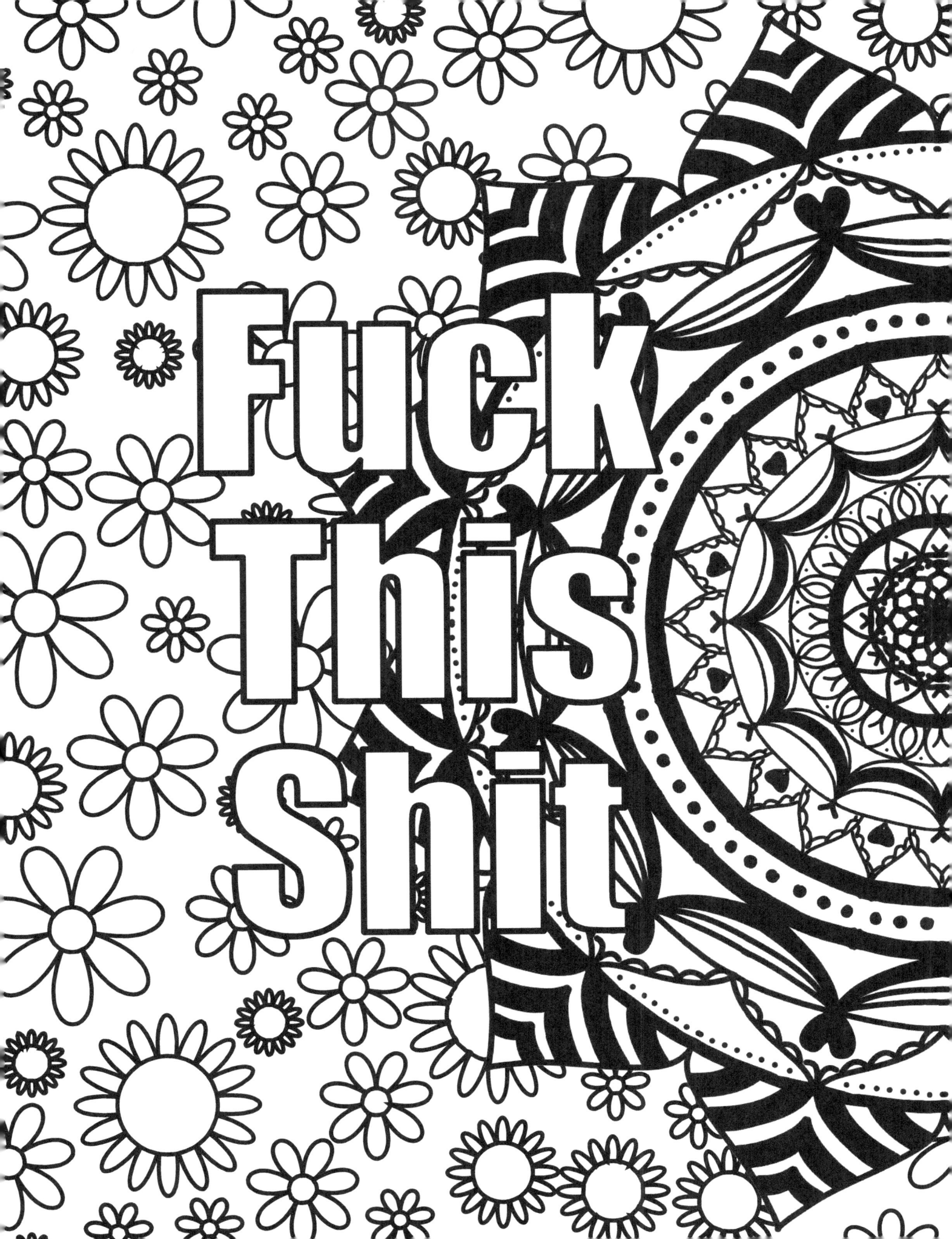

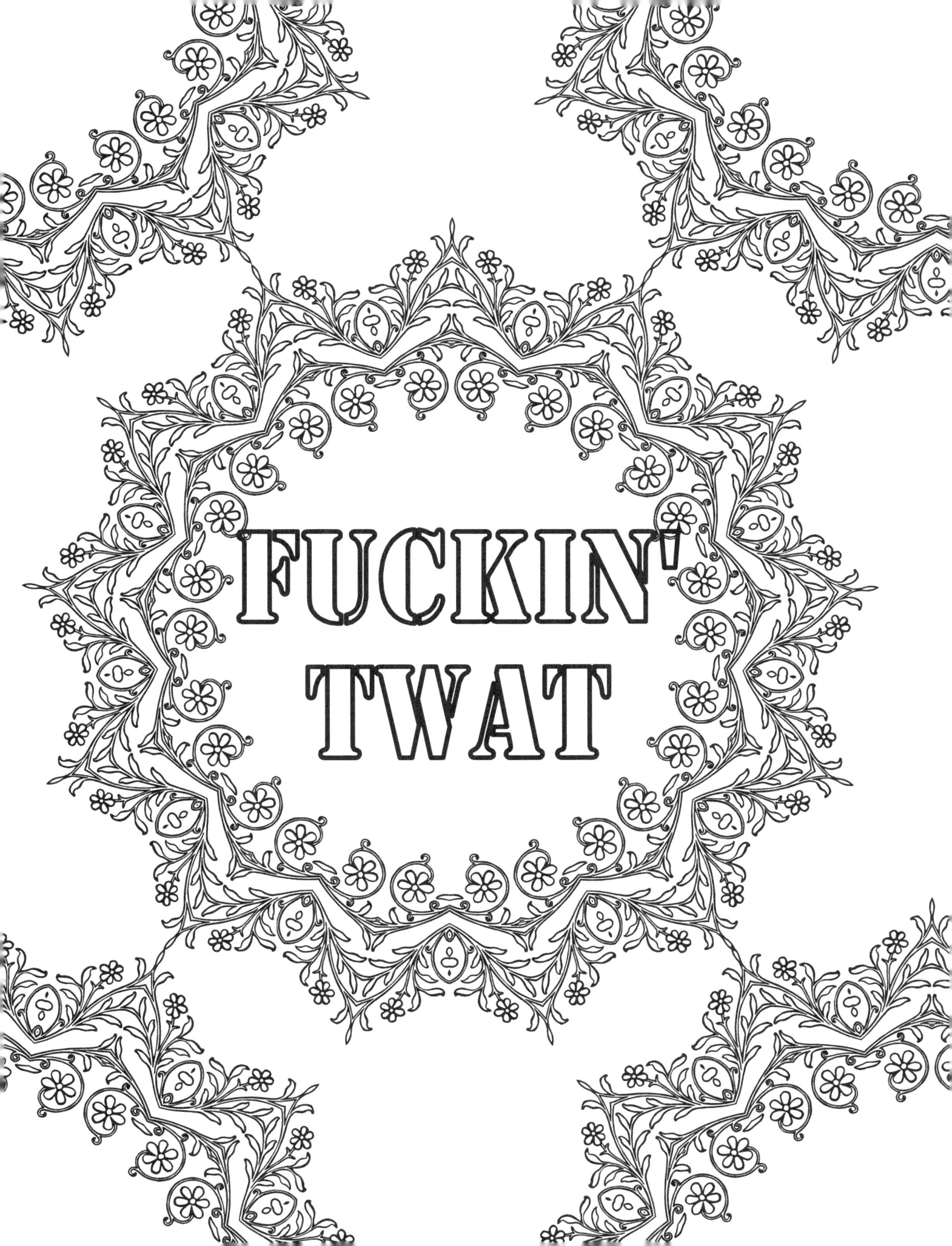

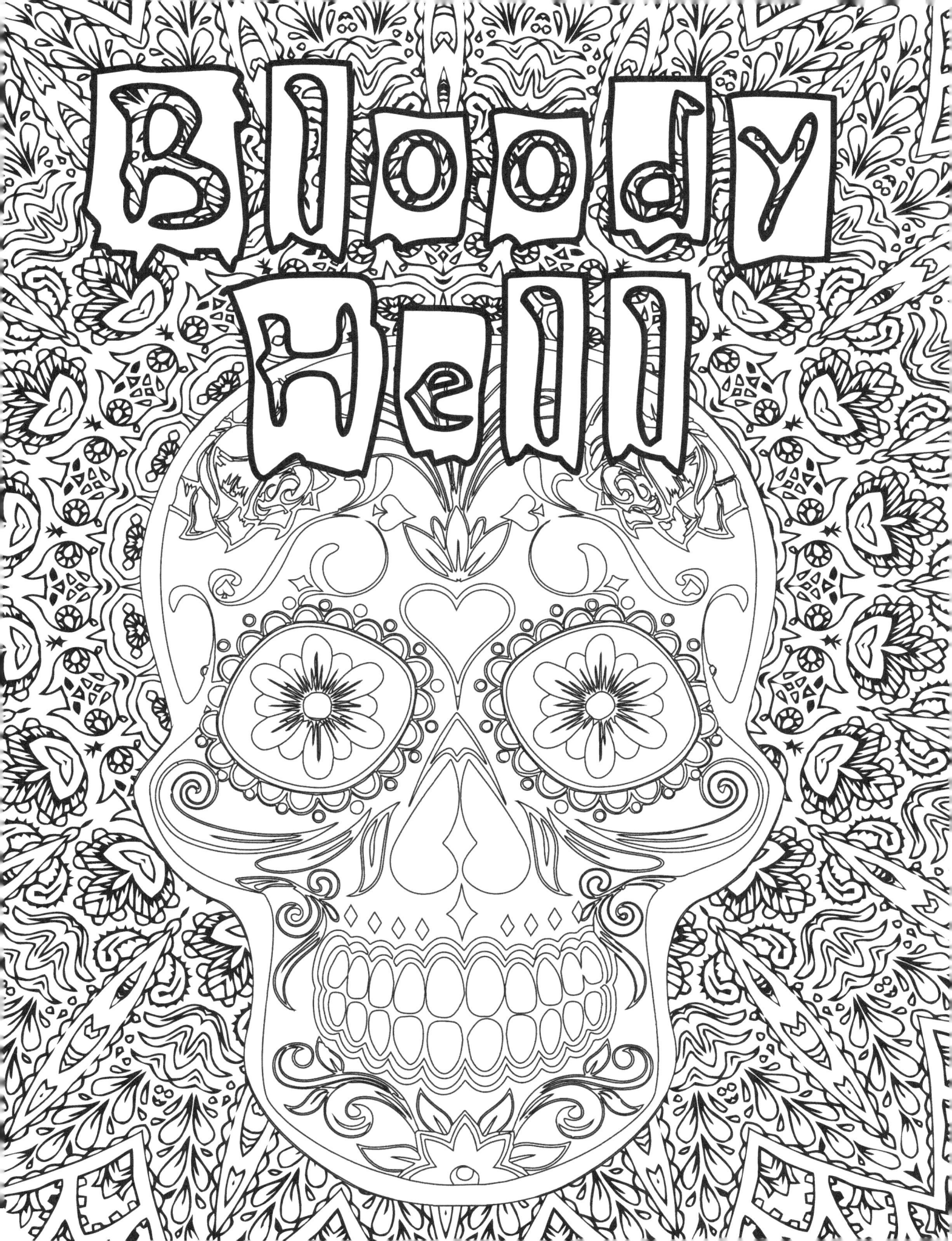

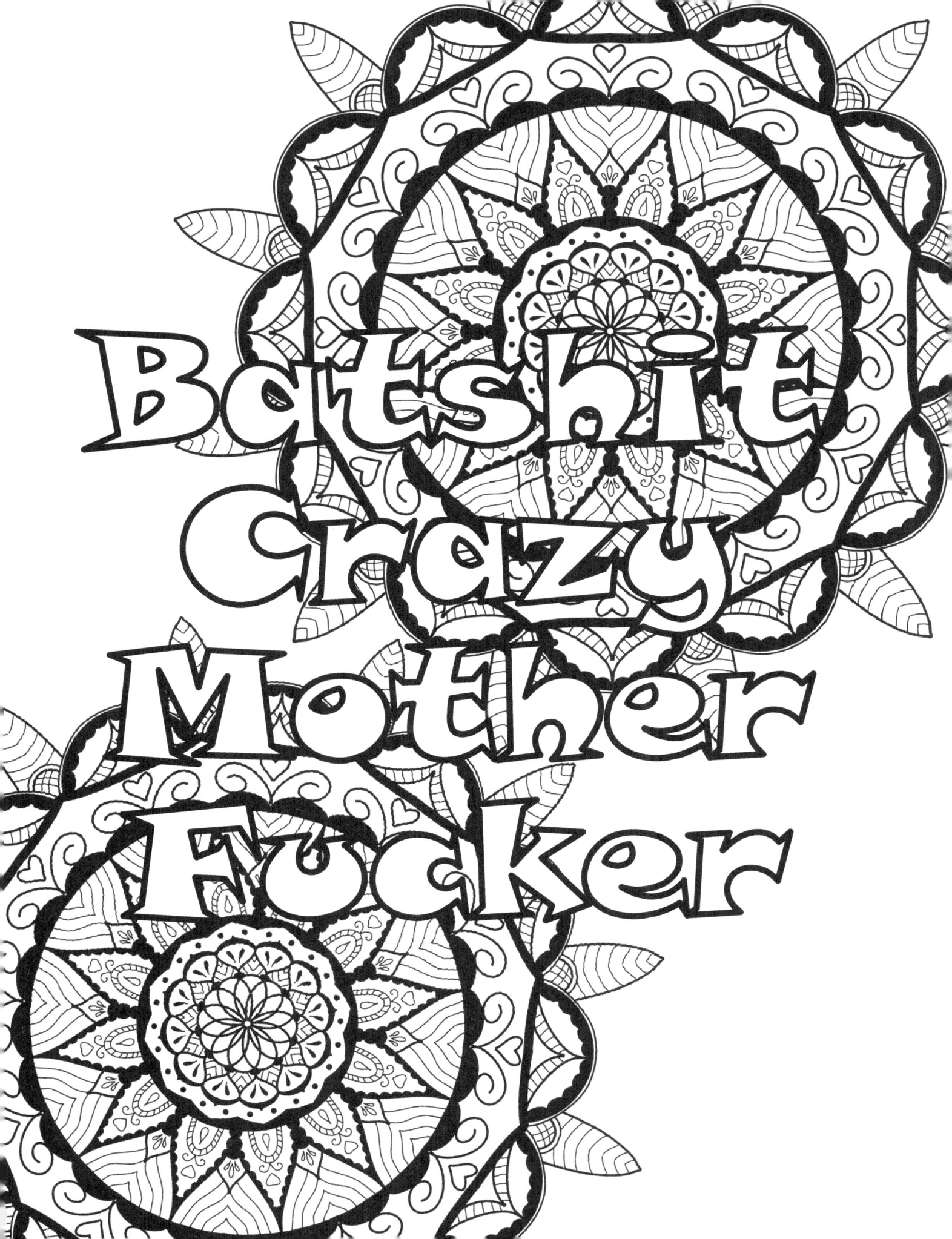

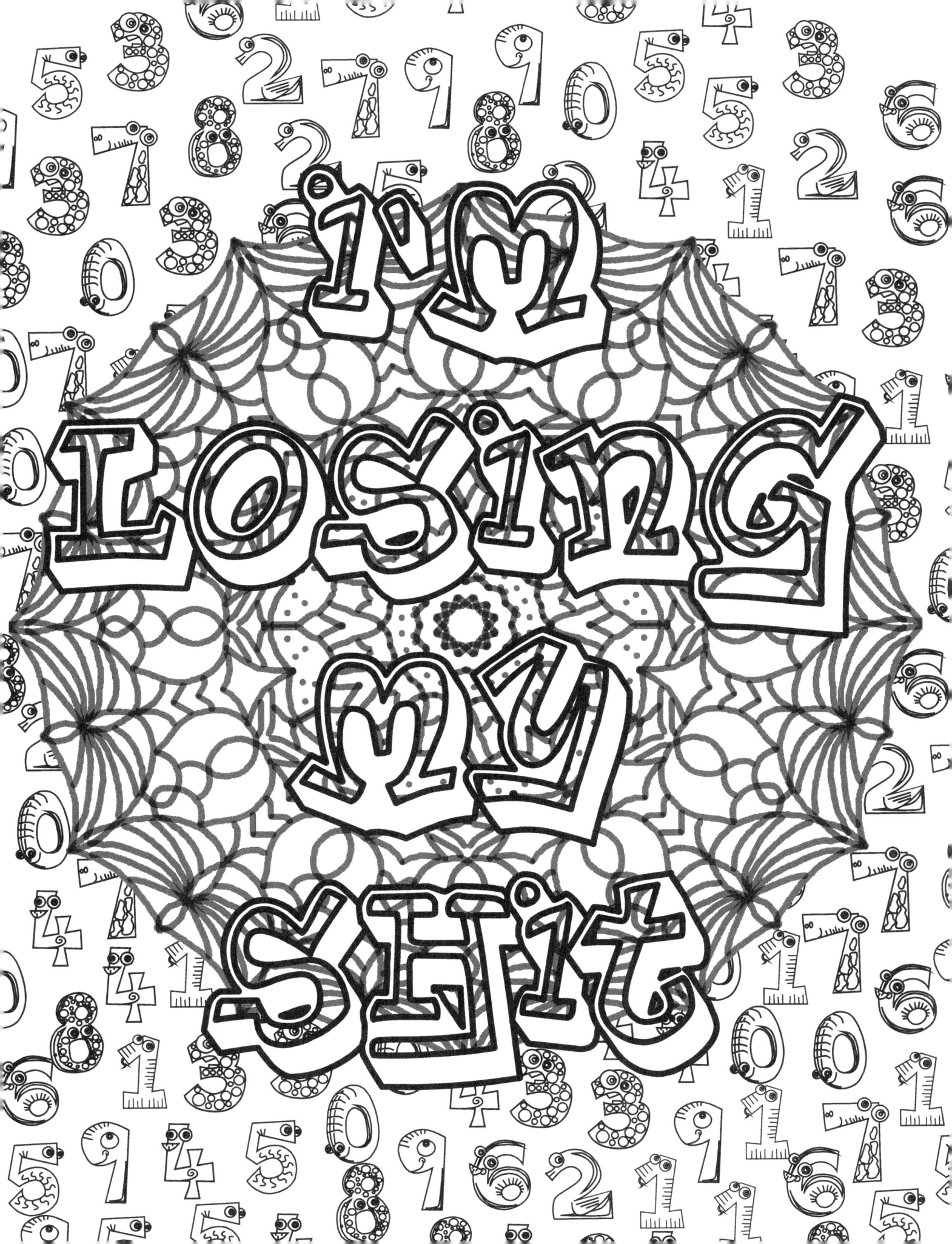

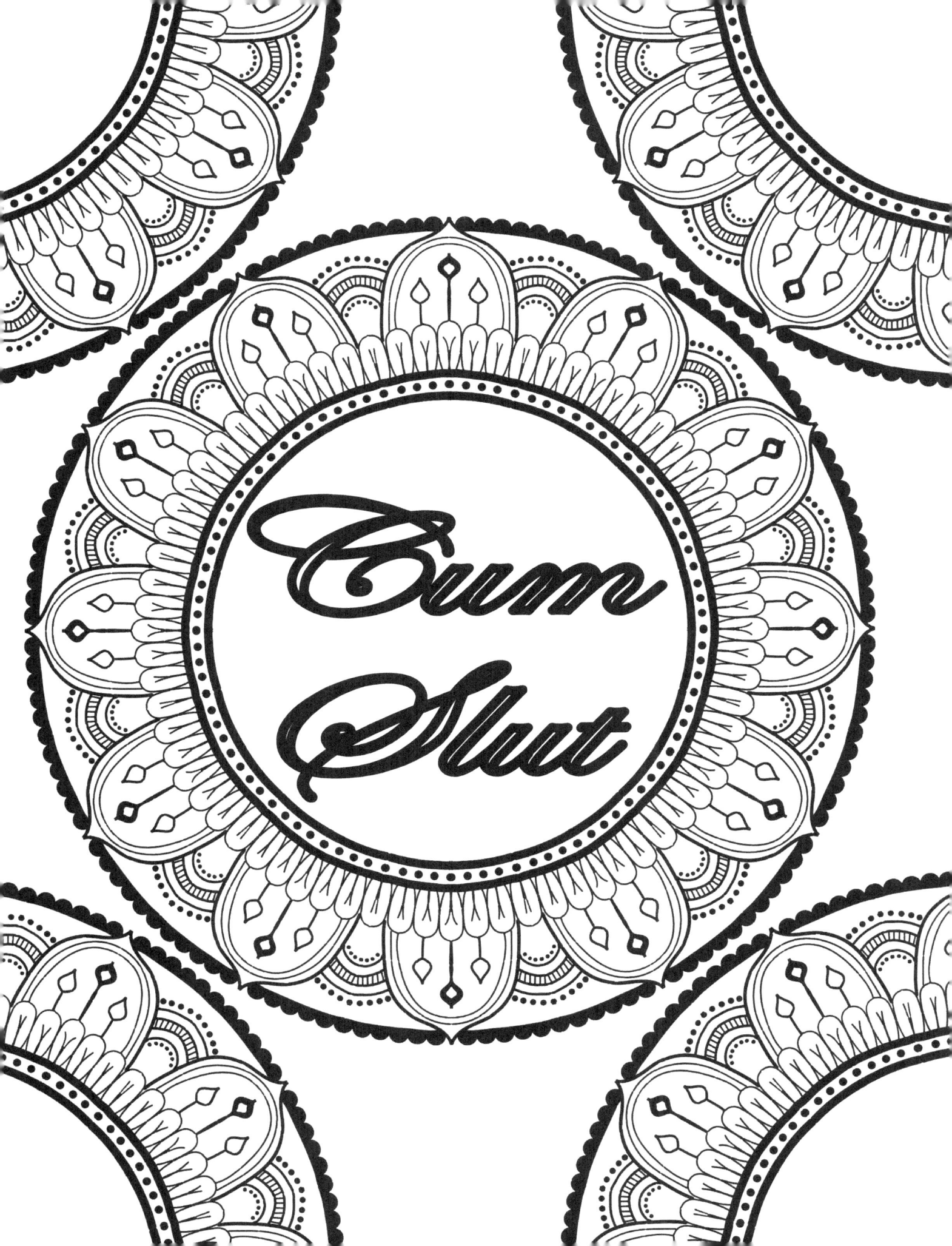

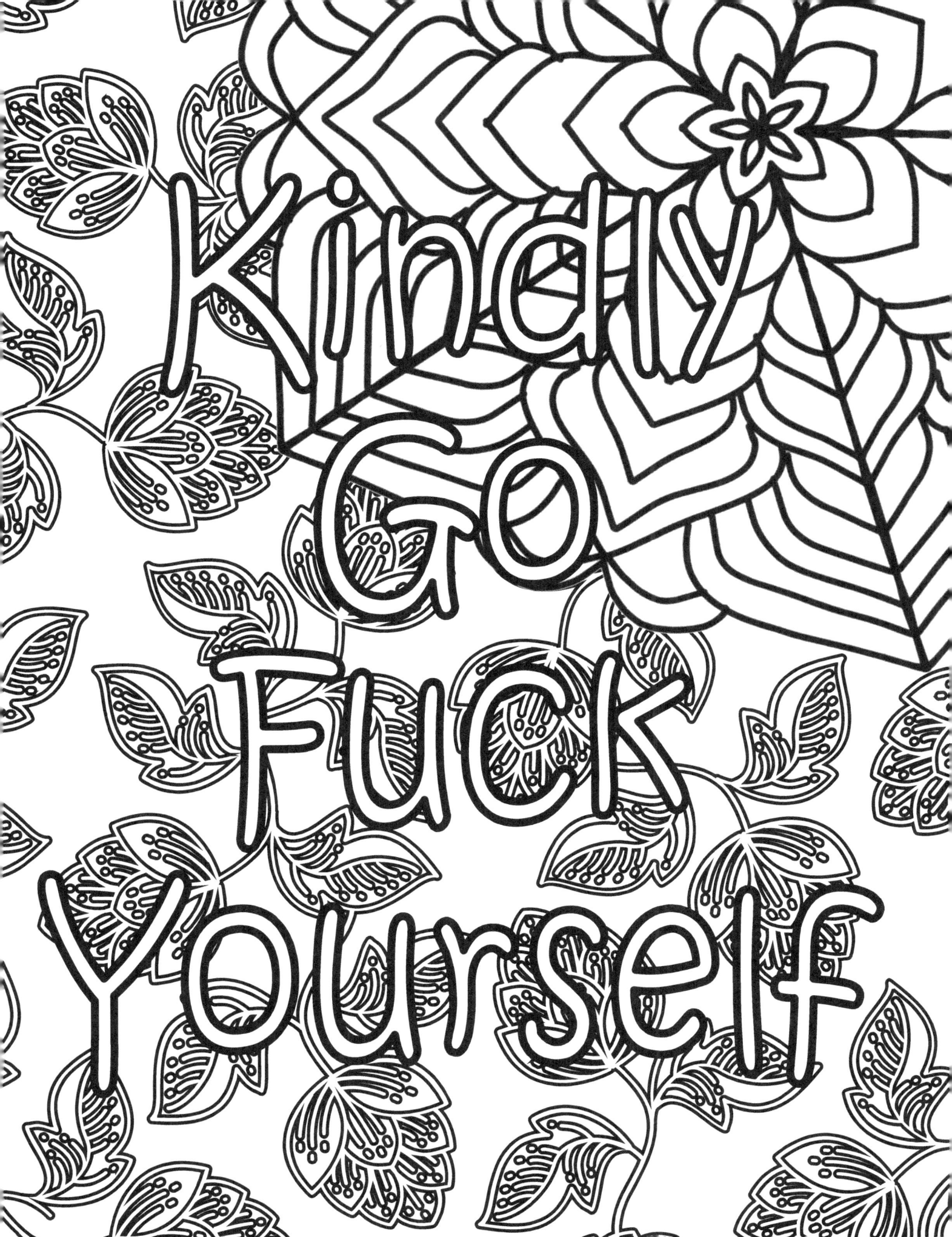

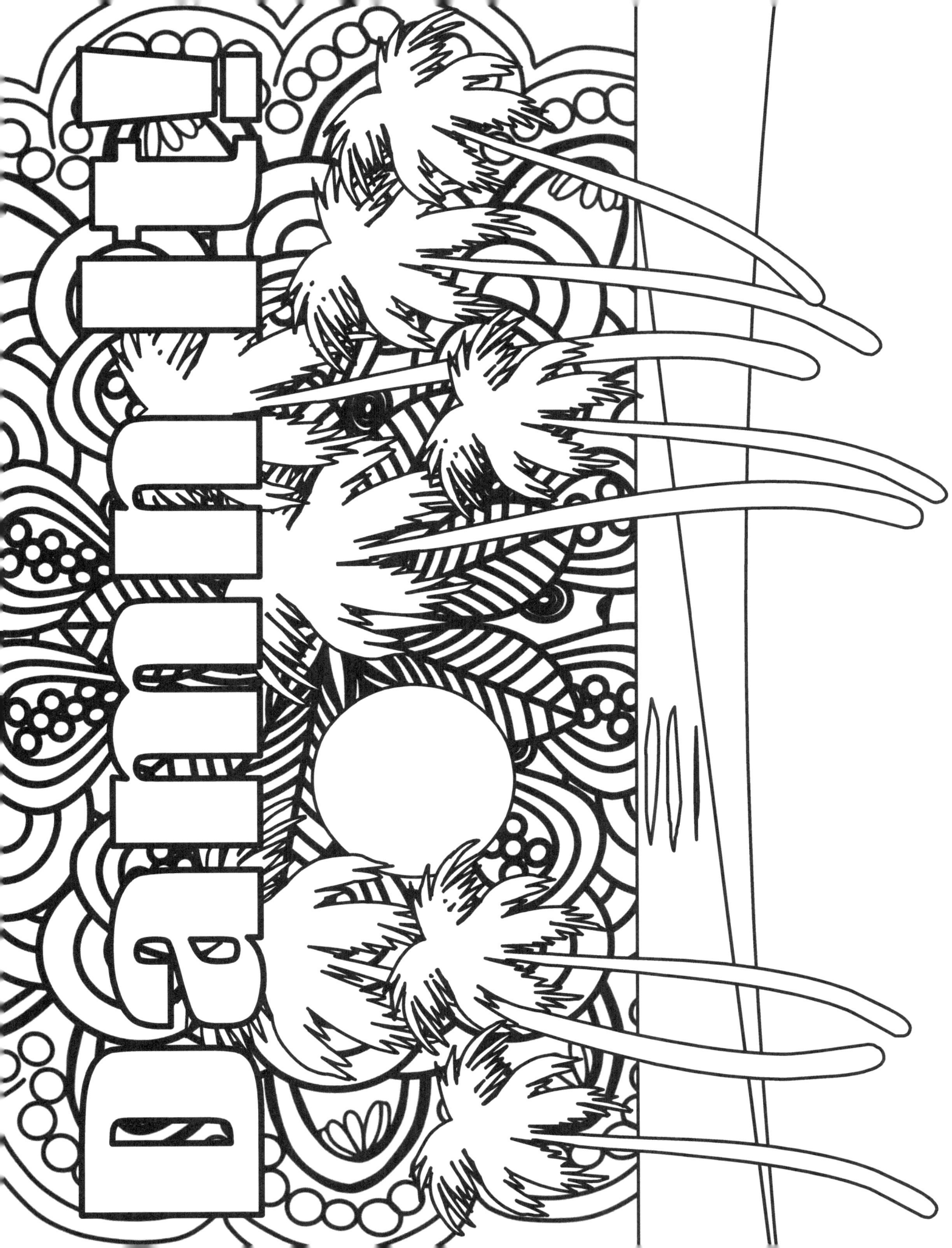

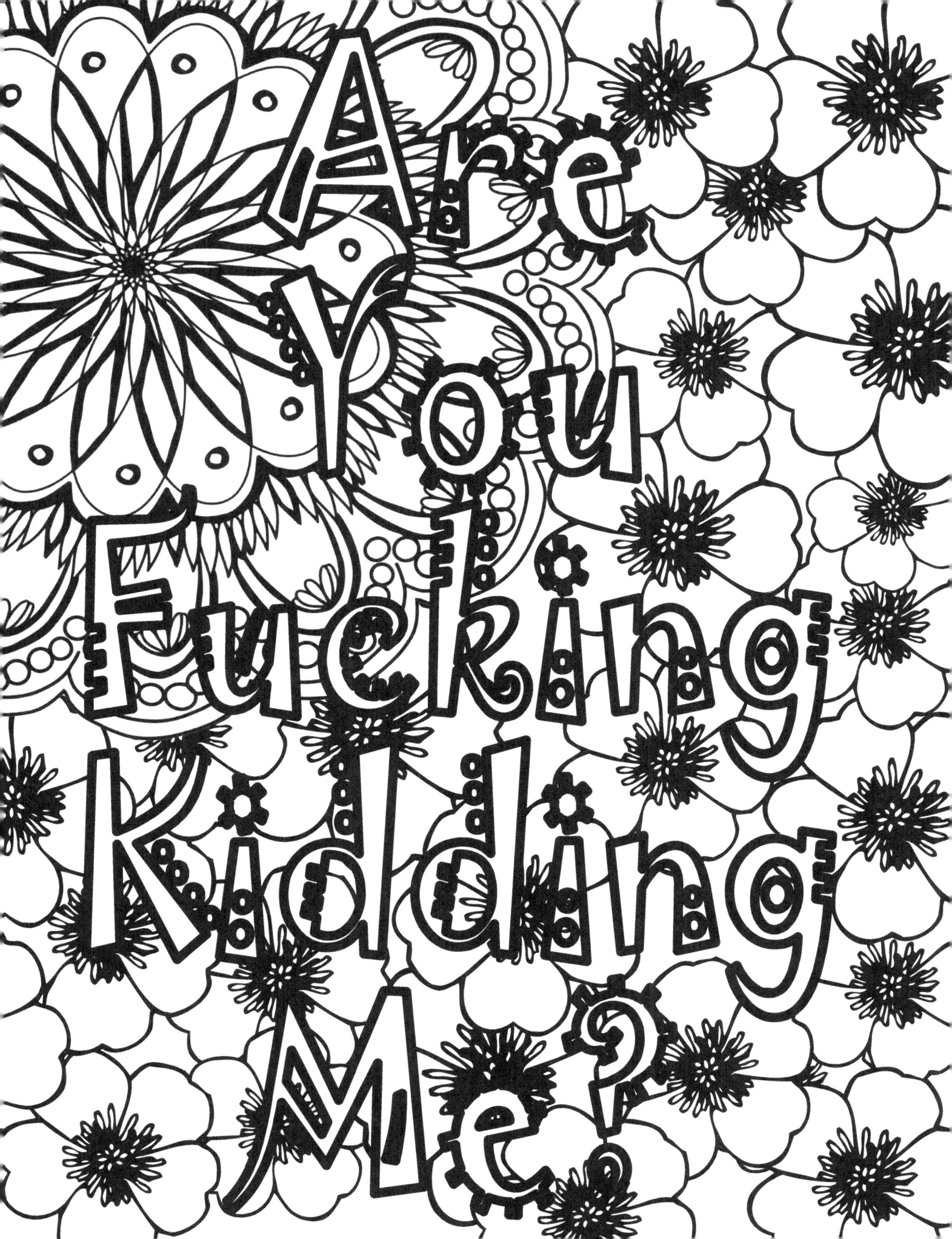

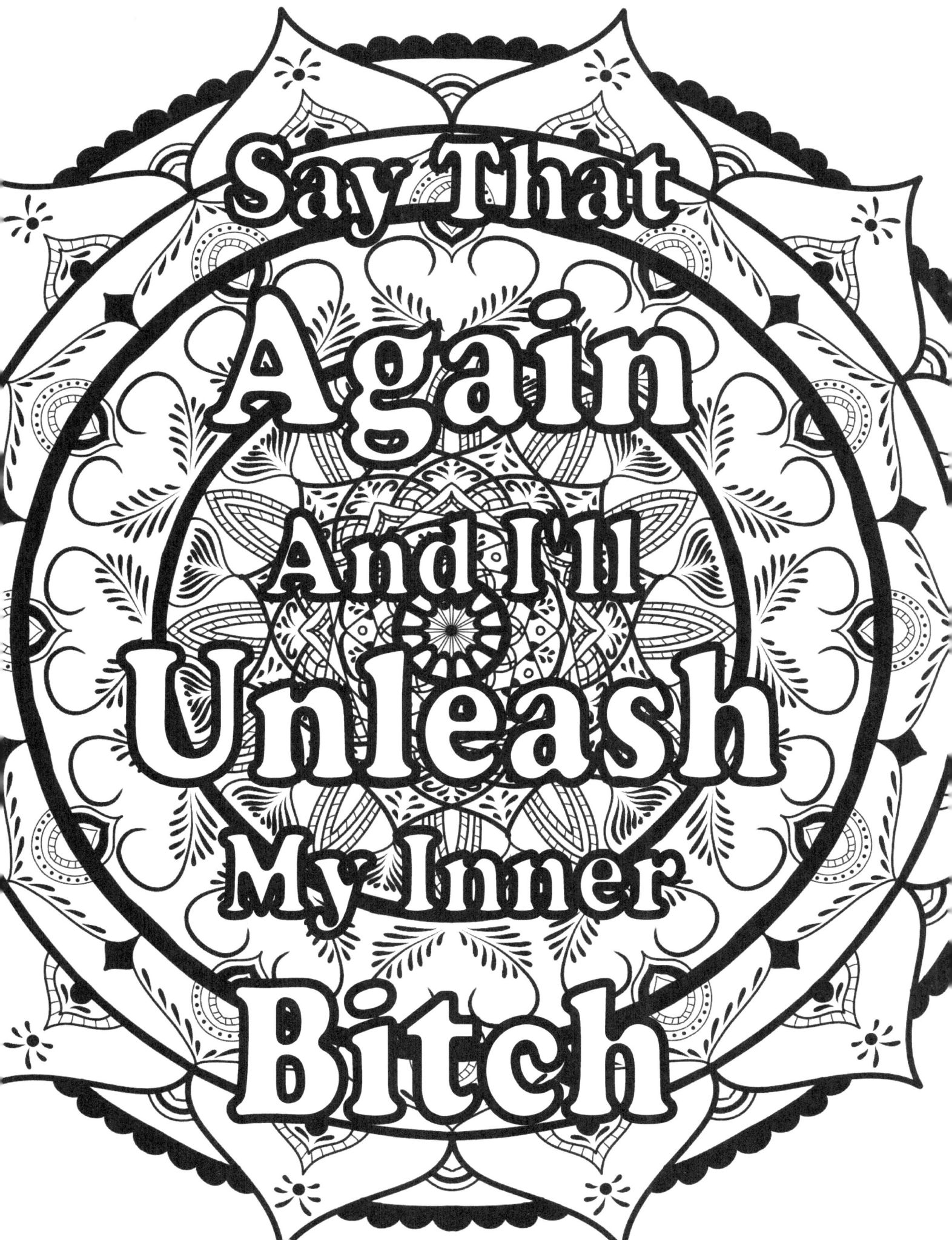

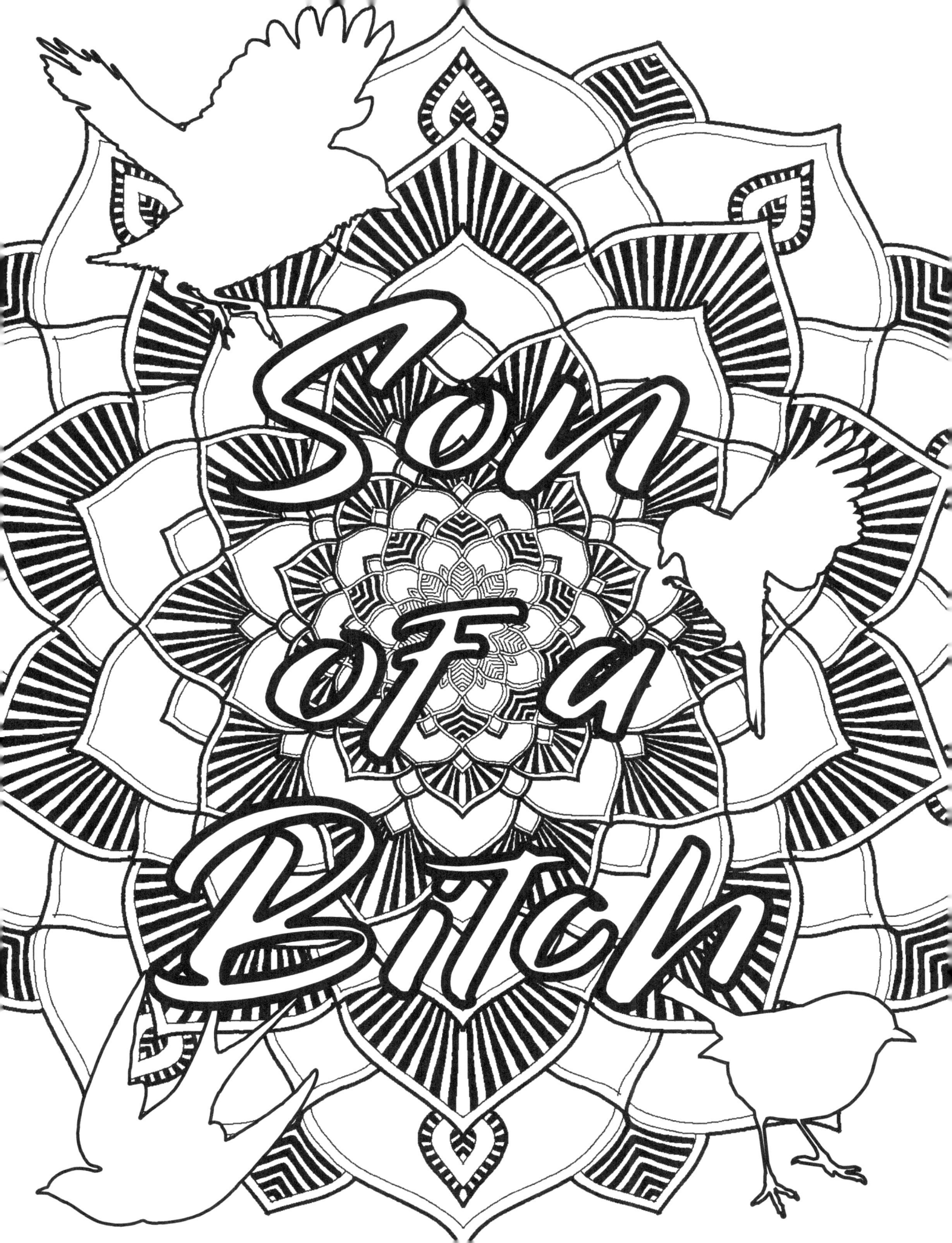

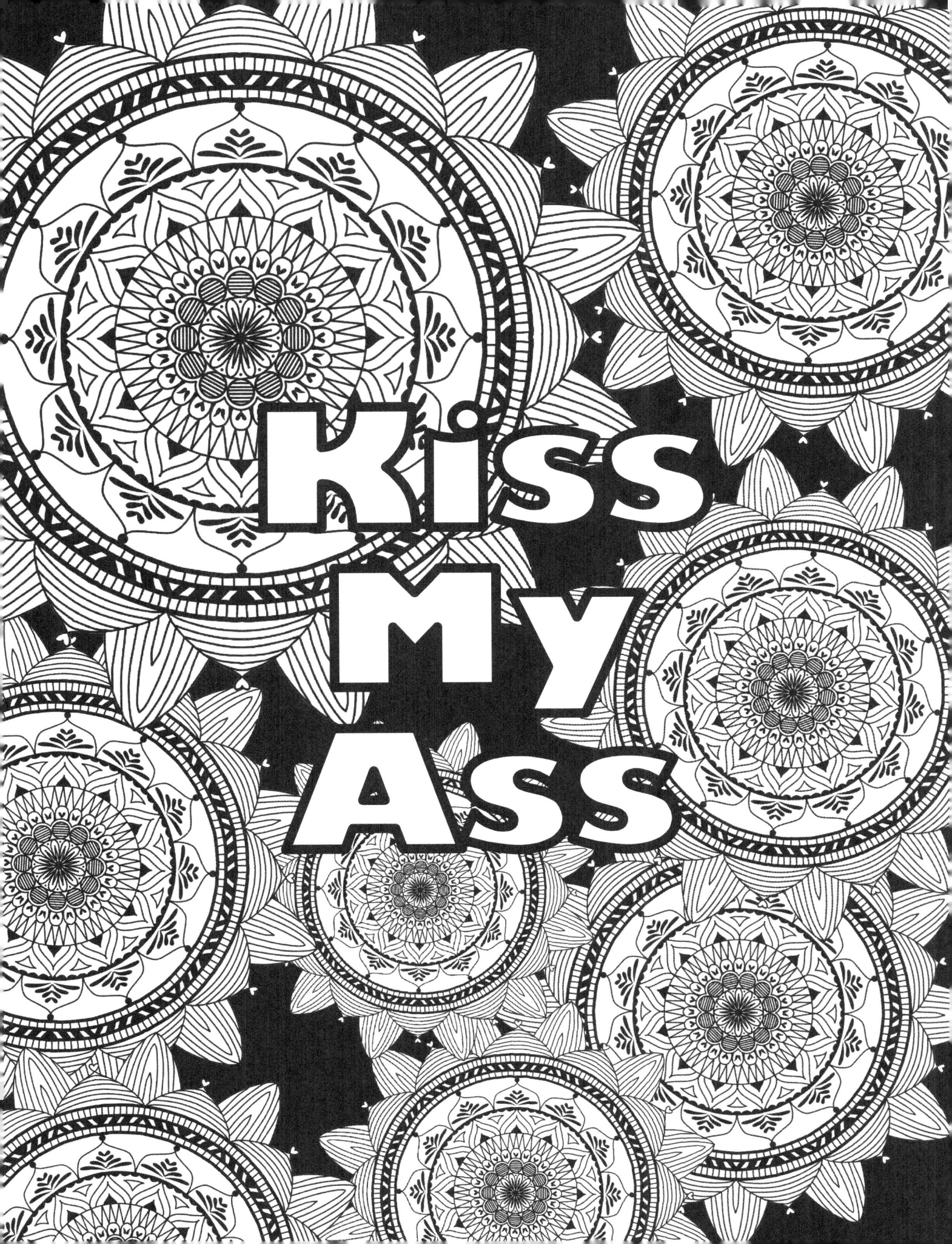

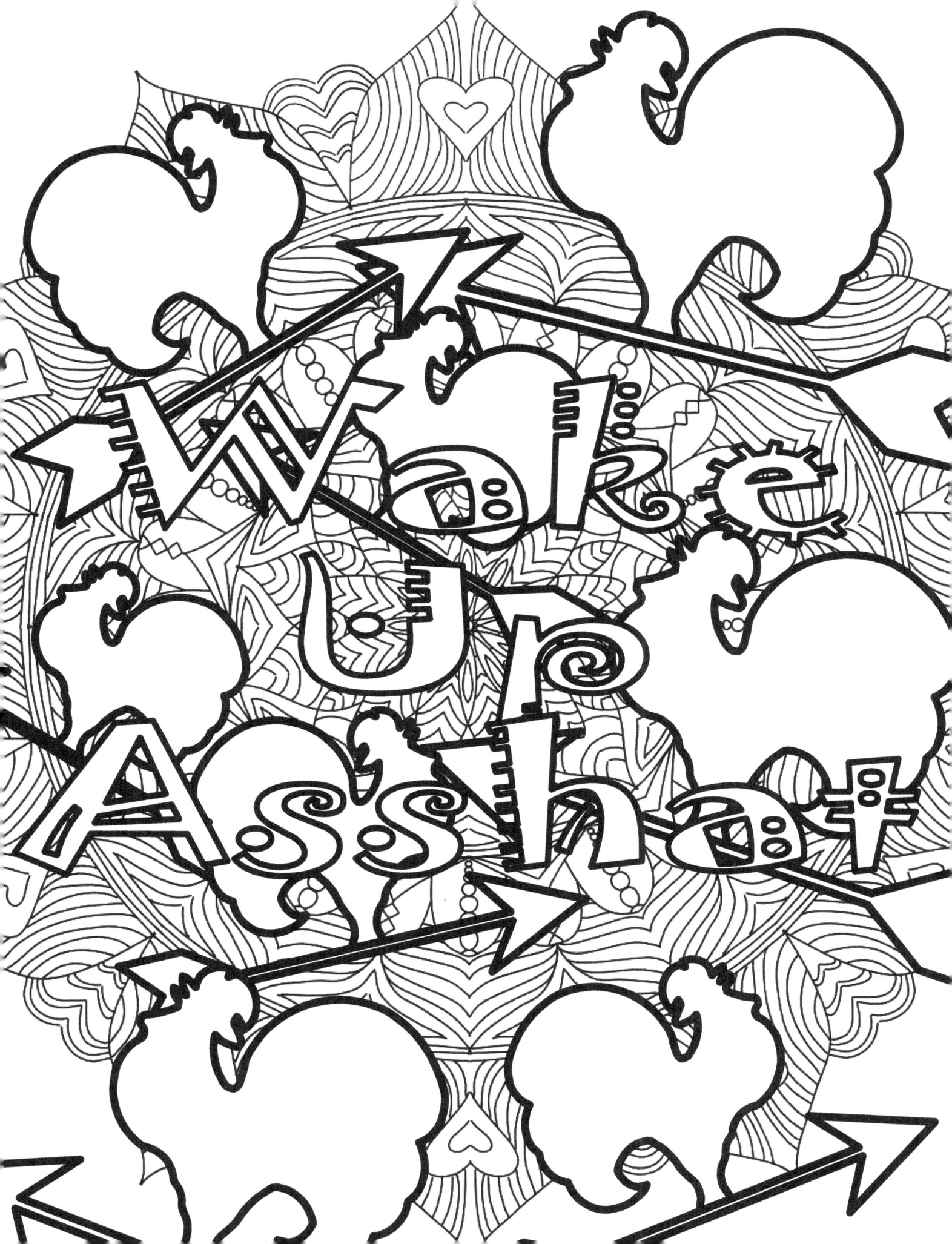

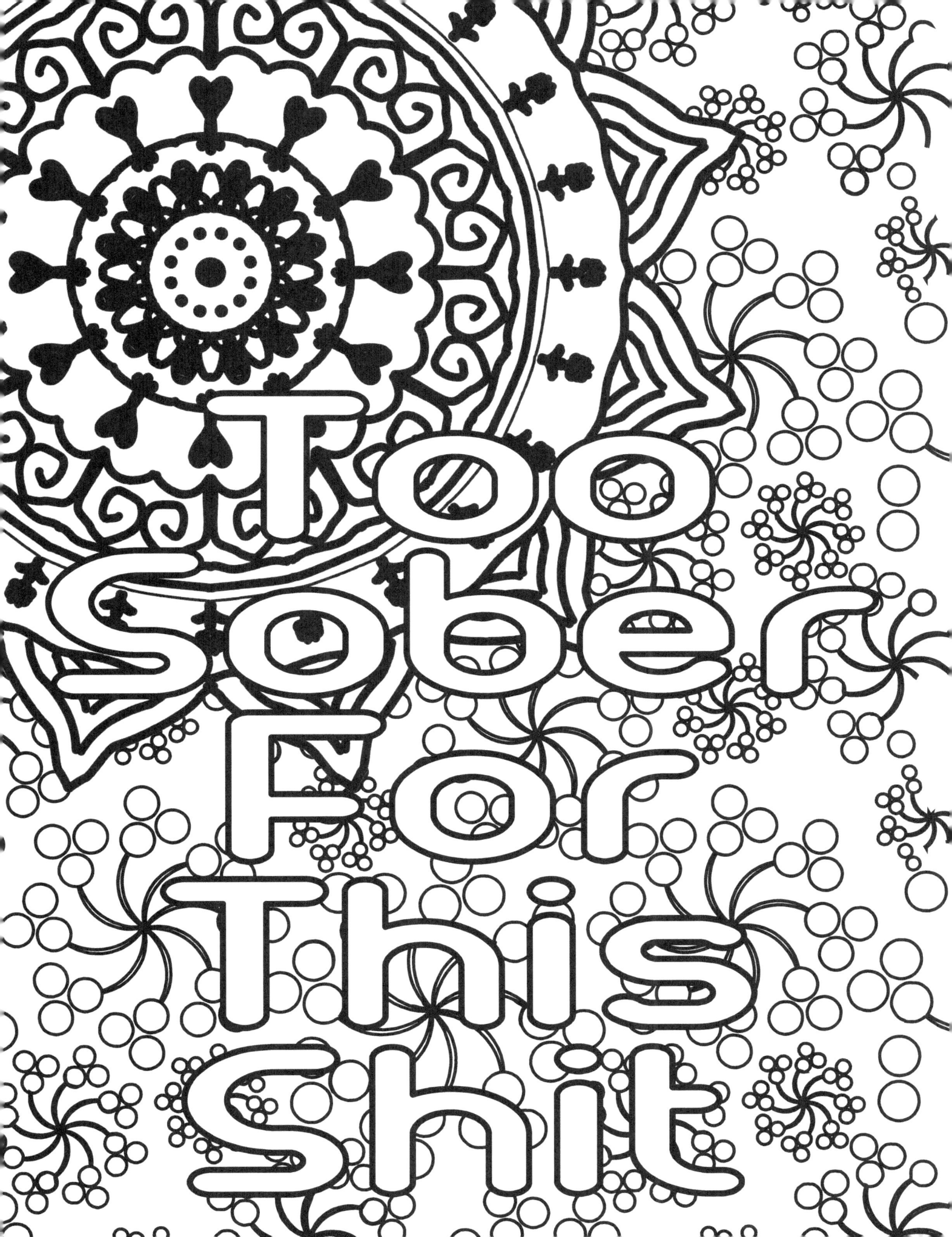

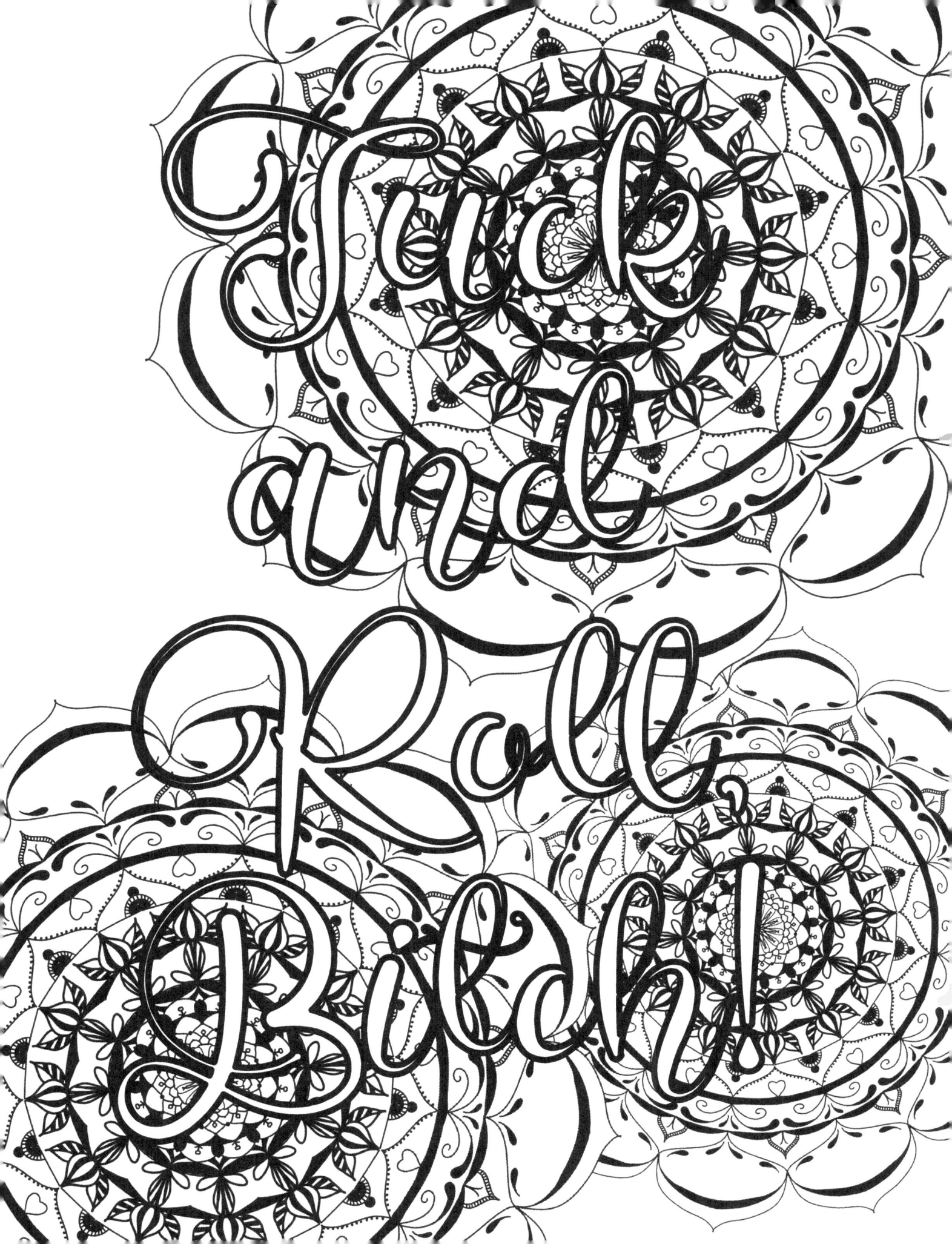

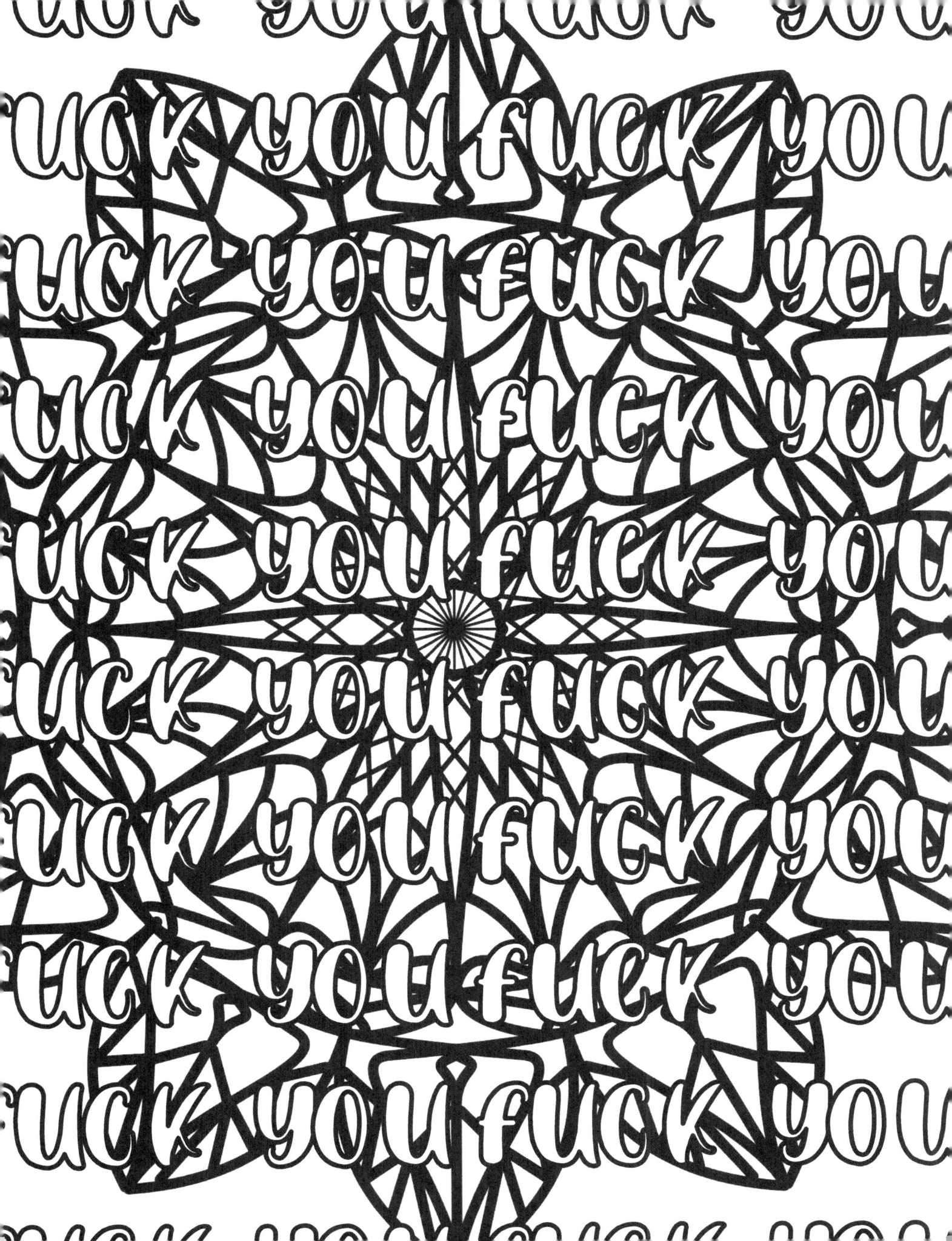

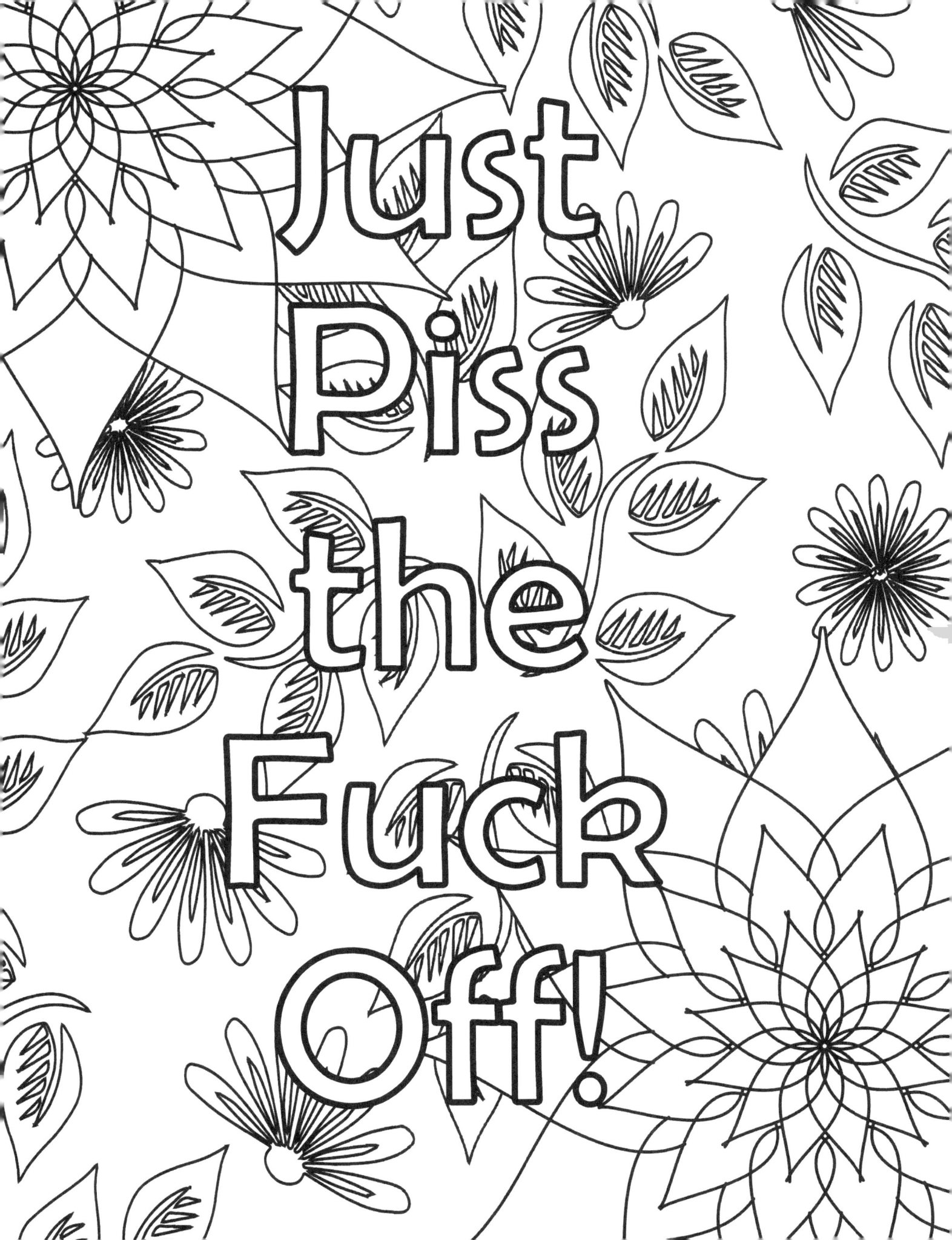

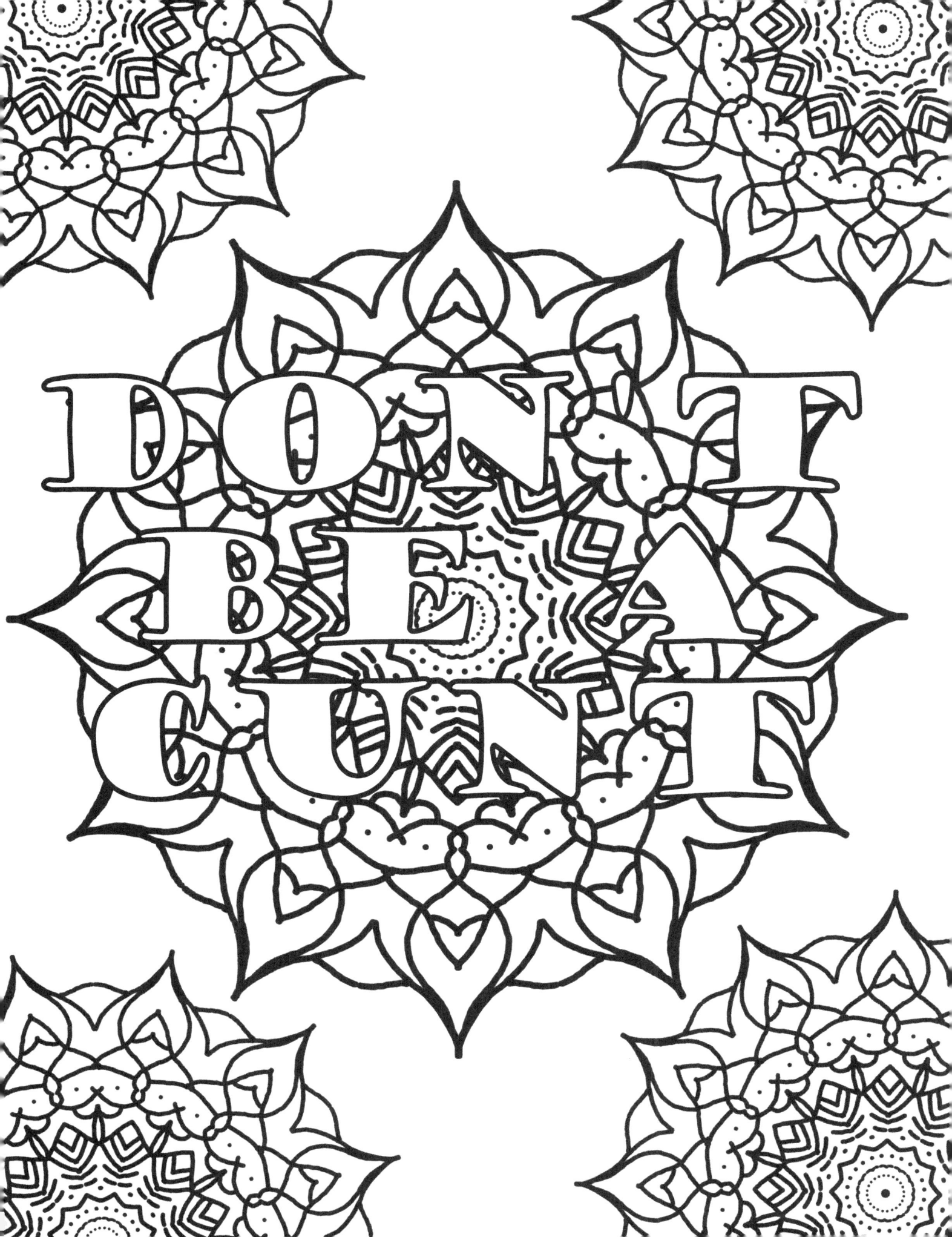

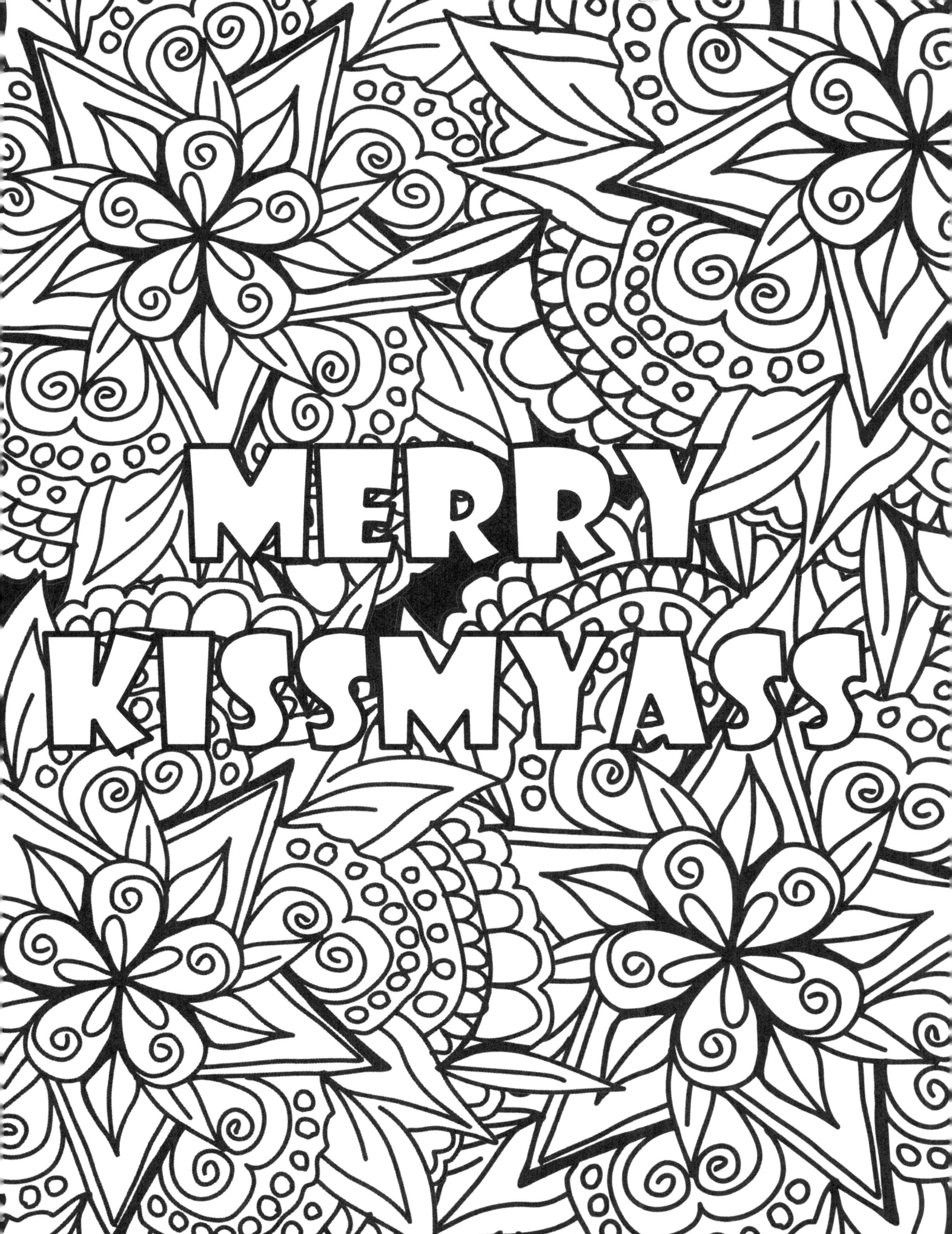

# Fucktard

# Color Test Page

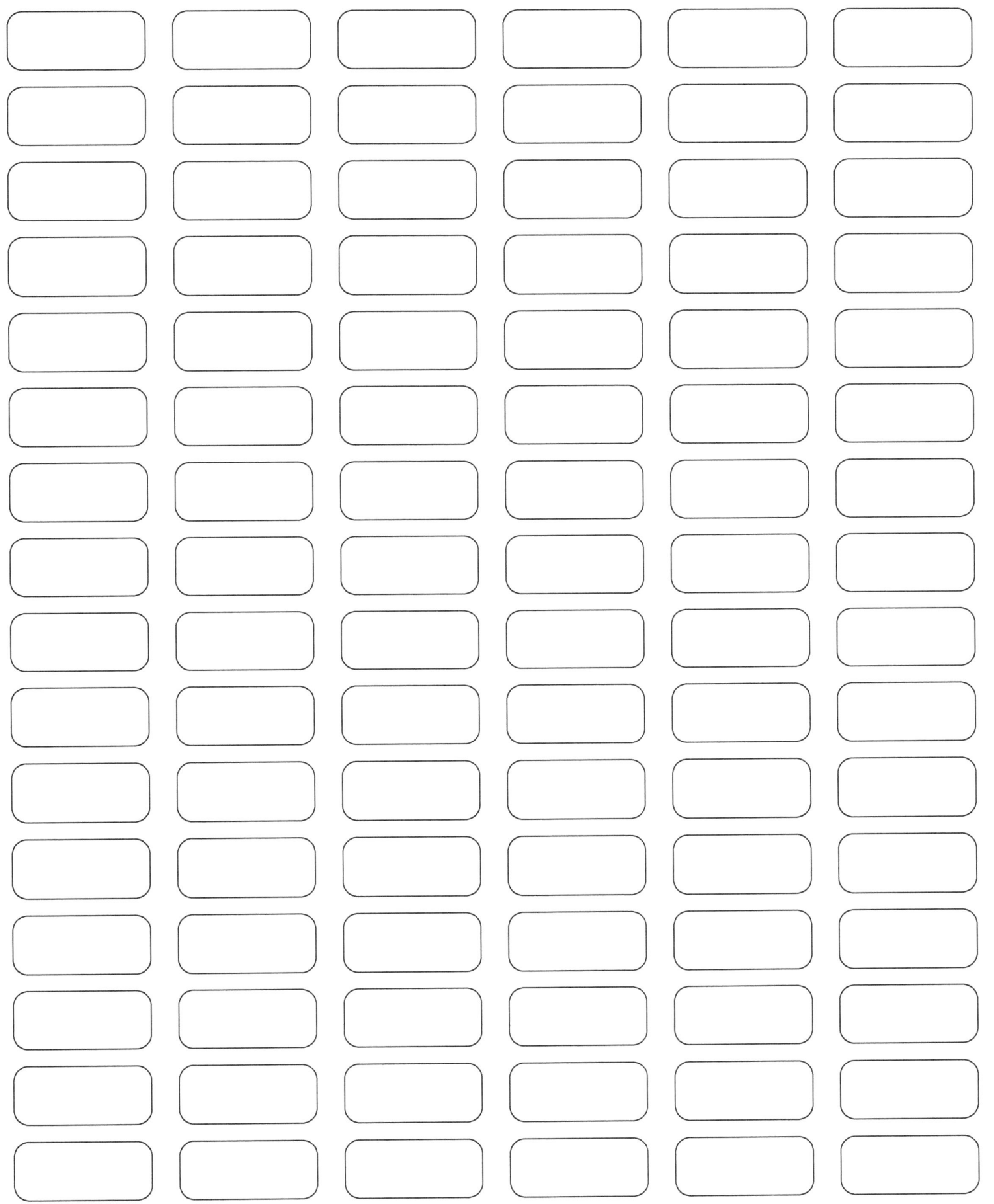

# Color Test Page

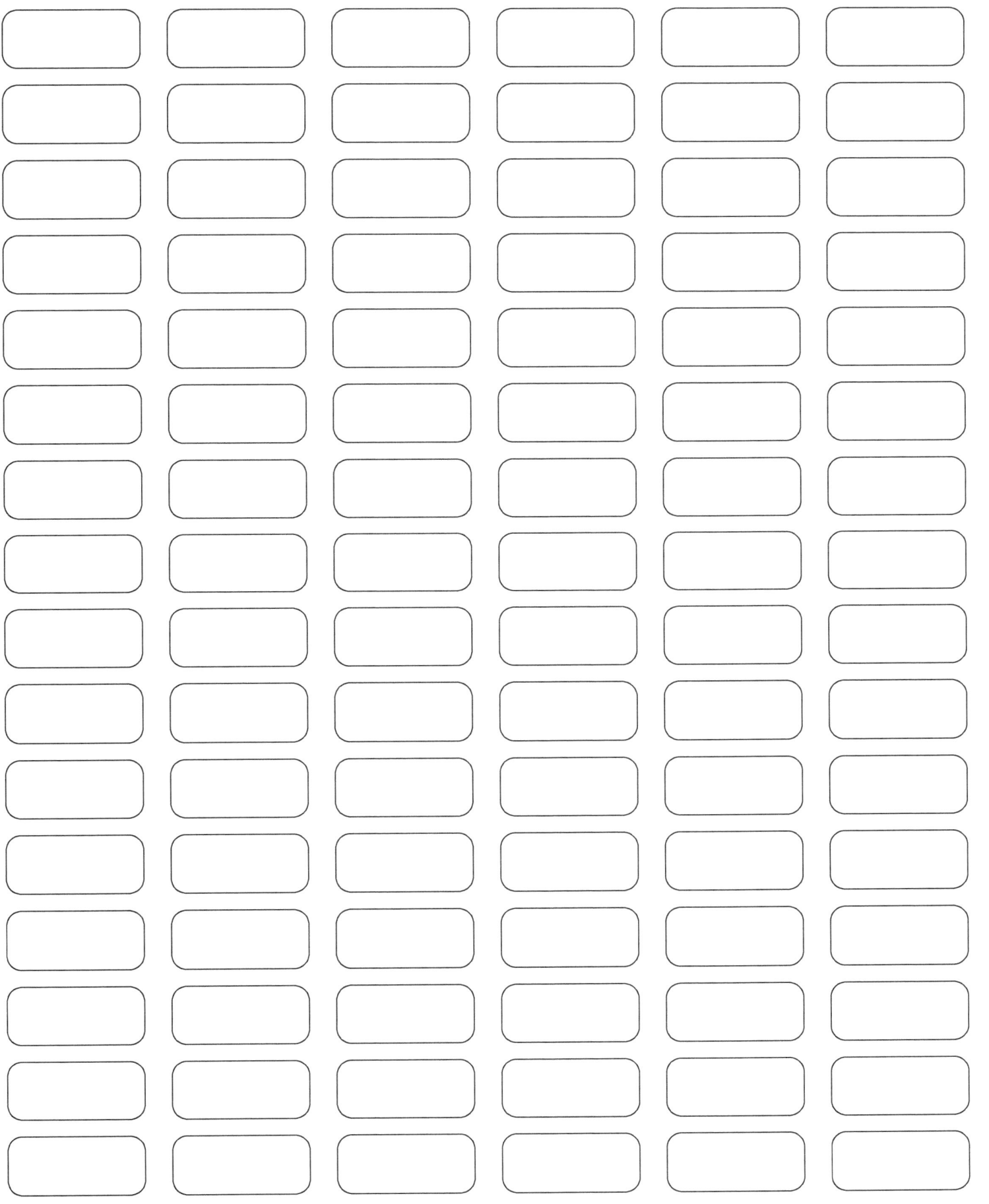

www.ingramcontent.com/pod-product-compliance
Lightning Source LLC
Chambersburg PA
CBHW060439220526
45465CB00008B/3205